STEPS TO SMALL BUSINESS START-UP

Everything You Need to Know to Turn Your Idea into a Successful Business

4th Edition

Linda Pinson / Jerry Jinnett

DEARBORN™
A **Kaplan Professional** Company

155 North Wacker Drive, Chicago, Illinois 60606-1719
(312) 836-4400   http://www.dearborn.com

Acquisitions Editor: Mary B. Good
Managing Editor: Jack Kiburz
Interior Design: Eliot House Productions
Cover Design: Scott Rattray, Rattray Design
Typesetting: Eliot House Productions

© 1983, 1987, 1993, 1996, and 2000 by Linda Pinson and Jerry Jinnett

Published by Dearborn, a Kaplan Professional Company

Printed in the United States of America

00 01 02 10 9 8 7 6 5 4 3 2 1

Library of Congress Cataloging-in-Publication Data
Pinson, Linda.
    Steps to small business start-up: everything you need to know to turn your idea into a successful business/Linda Pinson and Jerry Jinnett.—4th ed.
        p.   cm.
    Includes bibliographical references and index.
    ISBN 1-57410-132-3
    1. New business enterprises—United States. 2. Small business—United States. 3. Success in business—United States.
    I. Jinnett, Jerry. II. Title.
    HD62.5.P565 2000
    658.1' 11—dc21   99-42096
                                                                                          CIP

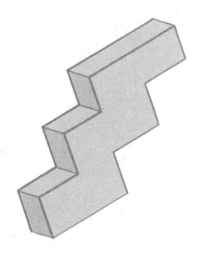

Table of Contents

Introduction

Now, more than at any time in our nation's history, the economy is being driven by the engine of small business. Hundreds of thousands of new businesses are started every year, and it is imperative that they are properly launched and given every chance to establish their niches in the marketplace of the new millennium.

We hope that you are pleased with our 2000 edition of *Steps to Small Business Start-Up*. This book has been written with the hope that it will provide you, the new small business entrepreneur, with the information, forms, and worksheets that you will need to go through the process of starting your business and laying a proper foundation for the development of a successful business venture.

We have tried to present the information in a logical sequence so that you will have a guideline to follow as you get your business organized and legalized. However, the procedures and requirements may vary slightly according to your location and industry. We would suggest that you read through the entire book one time and then go back and begin the process of forming your business.

Forms, examples, and worksheets have been included in the book for your convenience. They may be duplicated for your own use, but not for commercial purposes.

We have written *Steps to Small Business Start-Up* based on our experiences as business owners. We have also incorporated information and feedback from the many thousands of students, users of our books, and other small business owners with whom we have been fortunate enough to interact over the last several years.

We hope that you will benefit from this book and that it will provide you with the motivation and knowledge to take your idea "out of your mind... and into the marketplace."

Best wishes for a very successful small business.

—Linda Pinson and Jerry Jinnett

Acknowledgments

. . . .

Dearborn would like to acknowledge the works of Small Business Development Centers (SBDCs) around the country for their untiring support of start-ups and small business owners. Most notably, the Illinois SBDC Network has entered into a partnership with Dearborn to provide high quality materials such as *Steps to Small Business Start-Up* and other titles, to enhance the training and counseling of entrepreneurs in their state. This is the type of public/private partnership that will make today's small businesses prosper.

Other books and software by the same authors:

Anatomy of a Business Plan

Keeping the Books

Target Marketing

Automate Your Business Plan (software)

Getting Started

Everyone has dreamed of owning a business. At one time or another, we all have ideas that come into our minds but never quite make it into the marketplace. It has been said that an entrepreneur can best be defined by the following thought: all people have great ideas while in the shower. Most of us get out of the shower and forget about them. The entrepreneur is the person who gets out of the shower and acts on those ideas. However, you will increase your chances of success if you ask some tough questions before acting. What is my reason for starting a business? What type of business can I start? What skills, interests, and personal qualities will I be able to bring to the business? What are my strengths and weaknesses as a business owner?

◆ ◆ ◆ ◆ ◆

Examining Your Personal Objectives

Begin with examining why you want to start a business. People come to business ownership for a variety of reasons. They want to "be their own boss," "build a future," "follow the American dream," "earn lots of money." Look closely at why you want to start and run a business. What are your motivating factors?

There seem to be two schools of thought regarding business ownership:

1. Choose a business with great profit potential. After all, why would you go into business if not to make a lot of money?
2. Choose a business that you love. If you can't enjoy the work, why do it?

If profit is your motivation, take a close look at what that means. A business must be able to cover all of its costs, pay for all of its expenses, cover the owners' personal financial needs, and have enough net revenue left to allow the business to grow. Focus on the roll this business will play in your personal financial situation. Will this business provide you with a full income? Will the business supplement your current income? Before going much further, it is necessary to look at what your personal financial needs are. A **Personal Monthly Expense Worksheet** has been included to help you determine your total living expenses. This will help determine your **owner equity** or **draw** as explained on page 164, the **Cash to Be Paid Out Worksheet** for your business.

If doing what you love is your motivation, try to analyze what that means. Is there a market out there to support your dream? Is there enough potential revenue to make this a profitable business and not just a folly? Is your business feasible? Chapter 3 will show you how to determine the profitability of your business before you devote time and money to its development.

A successful business allows you to make a profit while doing work that you enjoy. With careful research and planning you can develop a business that fills a need, brings you pleasure and pride, and that will earn enough revenue to meet your personal needs, pay for itself, and provide profits for future growth. The key words here are **research** and **planning**. Continue with some research into what you, the owner, will bring to this business.

Exploring Business Ideas

Ideas for new businesses come from many sources. You may wish to turn an interest of yours into a business. Take a look at your hobbies, volunteer experience, and leisure activities. You could develop a line of specialty foods, do event planning, give golf lessons, or develop an antique locating and refinishing service.

Sell what you know. Any specialized knowledge or skill can be turned into a business. You can develop a newspaper column, write a book, present workshops, and conduct seminars in your area of expertise. An understanding of the Internet can lead to a business of designing, monitoring, and updating Web sites. This same knowledge can be used to retrieve information useful to other businesses. You can prepare demographic studies, databases, market surveys, and information resource lists.

You can put to work equipment and technology you already have. Desktop publishing, video recording of weddings, and photography of children's sports events are examples of businesses that make use of equipment you may already own and be proficient in using.

Many new businesses are started by individuals who utilize existing skills from their salaried jobs. Accountants, payroll administrators, technical writers, and computer specialists are examples of employees who have marketable skills that can be developed into service businesses. As companies **downsize** and **outsource**, new opportunities arise for entrepreneurs.

Any task or responsibility people don't like to do or don't have time to do for themselves can be the basis for a service business. House cleaning, home repairs, gardening, proofreading, gift purchasing, and furniture refinishing may fill needs in your business community.

You may wish to explore an idea that is new to you. Take classes, apprentice, or work in an area dealing with your new field of interest. If you think you might be interested in catering or some other facet of the food industry, work at a restaurant. Learn all of the aspects of the business. How are supplies ordered, how are deliveries handled, how is inventory controlled, how is food handled, and how are invoices and purchase orders handled? What are the strengths of the restaurant? What would you improve? You are not going to steal their business plan! You are getting an education while moonlighting and earning extra money to put toward the start-up of your business. You will learn to feel comfortable with the terminology and procedures of the food industry. You will also find out if you really enjoy working with food.

An inventive entrepreneur can develop a new product or improve an existing one. Now is the time for the old adage, "find a need and fill it." New products are usually spawned out of the imagination. If you can't think of something new, remember that many existing products can be improved on. A welder we know has designed an improved version of a jack used for leveling mobile homes. He used his creative talent in designing the new jack and his welding skill in manufacturing his product. He has created a double need for his talents. His product is timely and today he is a busy, happy, and prosperous man.

Identifying Skills, Interests, and Personal Qualities

Now is a good time to step back and take an objective look at what lies ahead. Business ownership is not for everyone. While some people may have the motivation and desire for business ownership, they may not have taken the time to properly investigate and research their abilities and their business ideas. A careful evaluation of your skills, interests, and personal qualities can help you determine the business you are best suited for. Skills are your abilities to use your knowledge and training proficiently. Interests are those things you enjoy doing and that bring you pleasure. Personal qualities are those traits and characteristics that make you unique.

Downsize: term currently used to indicate employee reassignment, layoffs, and restructuring in order to make a business more competitive, efficient, and/or cost-effective.

Outsource: term used in business to identify the process of subcontracting work to outside vendors.

Product: anything capable of satisfying needs, including tangible items, services, and ideas.

TECH TIP 1
Access Start-Up Information via the Internet

Technological advances enable you to quickly and easily access up-to-the-minute information on business start-up. The Small Business Administration's Web site at www.sba/gov is an excellent source of business information. Access the site and click on "Starting a Business" on the home page. Then check out "Your First Steps" and "Start-Up Kit." The latter provides a table of contents for the SBA Small Business Resource Guide. Clicking on individual topics will yield specific information on business development and the text contains hotlinks to additional sites and information. Through this site, you can also access special interest groups and electronic mail forums and you will find a searchable database of SBA publications and resources.

Another site of interest is maintained by the Edward Lowe Foundation at www.edgeonline. The site provides modules on all aspects of starting and growing a business as well as links to other resources. Browse the Edge Library for past articles or enter "How to Start a Business" at Search to be linked to numerous documents covering the start-up process.

When you are accessing information over the Internet, it is a good idea to "bookmark" key sites. The most useful sites are updated and changed frequently. The key article or information you find today may not be there tomorrow, so it is a good idea to download or print articles and information of use when first located.

A **Personal Assessment Worksheet 1** has been provided to help you analyze your skills, interests, and personal qualities and determine the types of businesses you may be suited for. Keep this worksheet within easy reach and fill it out as you go through your day's activities. You may have everyday skills, interests, and personal qualities that could be enhanced and utilized for business purposes. Do you have a mechanical ability? You might consider a repair service. Are you interested in arts and crafts? You can turn what has been a hobby into a full-scale business. Do you enjoy working with other people? If so, you could consider tutoring or teaching.

When you have completed the first three columns of the worksheet, you are ready to tackle the fourth column, **business possibilities**. This column is filled out by evaluating and combining the other three. For example, if one of your interests is dining out and you have writing skills, you could write and publish a local dining guide. If you are interested in collecting music boxes, skilled in mechanical repairs, and proficient at working with the public, you can provide a music box service combining repairs and sales. Extra emphasis should be placed on the area of "interest." You will be spending a great deal of time in your business pursuit and you might as well enjoy it. The ability to do well at your business may prove to be rewarding while the business is new, but if you do not like your work, it soon becomes a drudgery. Instead of looking forward to beginning your business day, you will be searching for ways to escape to more interesting diversions.

Evaluating Your Strengths and Weaknesses

Analysis of your skills may have indicated areas where you may lack an appropriate skill. You don't have to be an expert to start a business, but you must have a realistic understanding of your **strengths** and **weaknesses**. No business owner knows everything! A **Personal Assessment Worksheet 2** has been provided to help you with this analysis.

If you identify an area in which you will need help, remember expertise can be learned or bought. You can compensate for weaknesses by taking classes, hiring staff, or using consultants. When you have an idea for a type of business, take classes to learn all that you can about your chosen field. Find a job in your field of interest and get hands-on experience. Community colleges, the Small Business Administration, and Small Business Development Centers in your area will offer or can direct you to workshops and classes on business topics such as recordkeeping, marketing, financing, and business planning.

Just as you looked at your strengths and weaknesses as a business owner, you must look at the strengths and weaknesses of your business idea. Do this before you quit your job, invest your money, or spend your time in starting the new business. When you have decided on a business, answer the following questions:

- ◆ Do you have the skills needed to run this business?
- ◆ Do you know what help you will need and where you will find that help?
- ◆ Do you have the time required to learn what you need to know?
- ◆ Can you afford the money needed to hire staff or to pay consultants?
- ◆ Are you genuinely interested in this particular business?
- ◆ Are you committed to the business's success?
- ◆ Are you willing to devote the time needed to develop a successful business?
- ◆ Does this business fill an unmet need?
- ◆ Is there a sufficient consumer demand to support your business?
- ◆ Can you effectively compete in the marketplace?
- ◆ Will you be able to understand your business financial statements such as cash flow, profit and loss, and balance sheet?
- ◆ Are you developing a business plan that you can use throughout the life of your business?

To be the owner of a successful business venture, you must be able to answer "yes" to all of these questions. Research business ideas and see

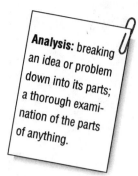

Analysis: breaking an idea or problem down into its parts; a thorough examination of the parts of anything.

Invest: to lay out money for any purpose from which a profit is expected.

Financial statements: documents that show your financial situation.

how they fit with your personality and background. Use the worksheets at the end of this chapter. Look at your skills, interests, and personal qualities in an objective manner. Then look at your strengths and weaknesses. Plan ways of overcoming your weaknesses. If this involves taking classes or hiring consultants or employees, calculate both the cost and the time involved. The costs incurred must be included in your **Cash to Be Paid Out Worksheet** in Chapter 17. You may wish to delay the start of your business until you have gained the knowledge and help you need.

Stepping Along

Now that you have identified a type of business you would like to develop, let's look at the various alternatives available to you. Chapter 2 will help you look at the advantages and disadvantages of starting up a new business, buying an existing business, and buying into a franchise. Once you have a business idea and your start-up format, Chapter 3 provides information on evaluating the profitability or feasibility of the potential business.

Personal Monthly Expense Worksheet

Regular Monthly Payments	Column 1	Personal Expenses	Column 2
Rent/mortgage payments		Clothing/shoes	
Property taxes		Cleaning/laundry	
Insurance: Homeowners		Education/training	
Renters		Subscriptions/books	
Life		Medical/dental care	
Health		Prescriptions	
Vehicle		Eating out	
Other		Travel	
Credit card payments:		Entertainment	
Groceries		Gifts/contributions/donations	
Childcare		Other	
Car expenses (gas, oil, etc.)			
Car payments			
Other loan payments		**Savings/Investments**	
Other payments			
Household Operating Expenses		**Column 2 Total**	
Telephone			
Gas		**Total Monthly Expenses (A):** **(total columns 1 + 2)**	
Electricity		**Total Monthly Outside Income (B):(non-business)**	
Water and sewer		**A – B = Minimum income needed from the business**	
Household maintenance/repair			
Household supplies			
Other			
Column 1 Total			

Personal Assessment Worksheet 1

Skills	Interests	Personal Qualities	Business Ideas
Organized	Sports	Enjoy meeting people	Sporting goods store
Can use computer	Fly-fishing	Independent	Teach classes
Writing skills	Reading	Self-confident	Conduct travel tours
Public speaking	Outdoor activities	Good work ethic	Write sports column
Good phone skills		Enjoy learning	
Communication skills		Decision maker	

Personal Assessment Worksheet 2

Strengths	Weaknesses	Action Plan	Cost	Time
Retail store experience	Lack of knowledge of business finances	Take basic accounting at community college	$65.00	6 weeks 4 hours per week
Managerial experience		Purchase Keeping the Books by Pinson/Jinnett	$22.95	
Worked as customer service rep				
Well known in community as an athlete	Don't enjoy financial work	Use an accountant	$50 per month	2 hours per month
Worked as a tour guide		Attend SBA workshops "Business Start-Up"	$20.00	4 hour class
Teaching experience		Contact local SBDC		
	Lack of knowledge of marketing procedures	Attend marketing class at community college	$85.00	8 hour workshop
	Lack of knowledge of writing a business plan	Work with a counselor from SCORE	Free	2 hours per week
		Purchase Anatomy of a Business Plan by Pinson/Jinnett	$21.95	
		Take Business Planning workshop from SBA	$40.00	8 hour workshop

Finding a Business

Starting and growing a business involves a great deal of decision making. In Chapter 1, you made a decision on the type of business you want to start. Now you are faced with three alternatives: start up a brand new business, buy an existing business, or buy a franchise. Each has benefits and drawbacks. Some of the differences in these choices are required investment capital, chance of survival and expected profit. Examine the advantages and disadvantages of each option before taking the entrepreneurial leap.

◆ ◆ ◆ ◆ ◆

Developing Your Own Business

There are advantages to developing your own business. Generally, it costs less up front to start a business than to buy one and you can make use of your creative talents in developing something unique. You can address unexplored markets. You are free to choose your own location and to develop your own management style and policies, and you will not be buying the problems and flaws of an existing business.

Most people who start their own businesses are good at what they do. They have used their talents and creativity to develop something unique. They manufacture, provide, or sell a good product or they provide a good service. But a successful entrepreneur has to provide a good product or service *and* understand how a business works.

There are certain inherent risks in developing your own business. You have to start from scratch. You are responsible for choosing a legal structure, a location, and a recordkeeping

Market: a set of potential or real buyers or a place in which there is a demand for products or services. Actual or potential buyers of a product or service.

Capital: money available to invest or the total of accumulated assets available for production.

Accountant: one who is skilled at keeping business records. Usually, a highly trained professional rather than one who keeps books. An accountant can set up the books needed for a business to operate and help the owner understand them.

system. You must get licenses and permits. You develop your customer base, your management and organizational systems, and your marketing plan. At times, this can seem overwhelming. The purpose of this book is to take the mystery out of business start-up. You will see that a business starts and develops in a logical order. Understanding how a business works is one way to increase your chances for success.

Buying an Existing Business

There are some advantages to buying an existing business. It may be the only way to get a good location in the area you want to do business in. You can save some of the time, work, and money that go into the start-up phase of business development. Often you are able to make use of the seller's invested capital. Many sellers will finance a large part of the sale for a lower interest rate than a lending institution would offer. An existing business already has an organizational plan and operating system in place. The customer base is already established. Often the seller will consult with the buyer on the management of the company.

There are a number of ways to find businesses for sale. Trade associations and neighborhood business groups are usually the first to know a business that is for sale and about the business's performance and reputation. Business brokers are a good professional resource for information on available properties, locations, markets, and financing. They can represent sellers or buyers and are paid a percentage of the sale price. The "Business Opportunity" advertising section of a newspaper will have local listings. Bankers, the chamber of commerce, and other professional people within the community often know people who are selling or are about to sell a business.

When you find a business you are interested in, determine why it is for sale. There may be serious business problems such as new competition, relocation of the primary customer base, obsolescence of a product line, or cash flow problems that have prompted the sale. Study the business and research its market carefully. Study the trends of the specific business. Learn about the competition, the surrounding neighborhood, the local business community, and the current customer base.

An experienced and independent accountant can help you analyze the seller's financial statements and tax records in order to determine profitability and purchase price. Do not take the word of the seller's accountant. Evaluate the seller's projections for future growth and performance. In an eagerness to sell, the owner might make claims that are overinflated. If you have difficulty getting the financial information you need, it might be wise to move on to another opportunity.

When you buy a business, you purchase a number of tangible and intangible assets. You want to know what you will be purchasing and

TECH TIP 2
Connecting with Other Business Owners

Some of the most valuable information on starting and running a business will come from people who have been there, done that; entrepreneurs who have started the same type of business you are starting. The Internet contains numerous newsgroups, chat rooms, and forums comprised of business owners who pose questions, share their experiences, and are ready to answer your queries. Discussion groups often are centered around a specific business topic and are led by experts in that field. While your local competitor may be reluctant to give out facts about start-up costs, pricing strategies, and sales figures, business owners from other parts of the country who are not threatened by your business will be much more willing to share information. Usenet is the part of the Internet that contains discussion groups and can be accessed through search engines. For starters, you might try the following:

AltaVista:	www.altavista.com
Infoseek:	www.infoseek.com
Lycos:	www.lycos.com
Yahoo:	www.yahoo.com
SmallBizSearch:	www.smallbizsearch.com

its current value before you set a price and close a sale. You want to know if any of the company's assets have been pledged as collateral for outstanding debt. It is wise to hire an appraiser to determine the value of the assets being purchased. These items may include the following:

- ◆ Accounts payable and other liabilities
- ◆ Accounts receivable
- ◆ Building
- ◆ Business name
- ◆ Business clientele and customer list
- ◆ Consulting agreement with seller
- ◆ Covenant not to compete
- ◆ Credit relationships
- ◆ Equipment
- ◆ Furniture and fixtures
- ◆ Inventory
- ◆ Lease agreements
- ◆ Liabilities and liens
- ◆ Personnel
- ◆ Trademark, copyright, patent
- ◆ Unpaid taxes

Assets: anything of worth that is owned. Accounts receivable are an asset.

Collateral: something of value given or held as a pledge that a debt or obligation will be fulfilled.

Inventory: a list of assets being held for sale.

A **Buying a Business Worksheet** had been included on page 17 to help you evaluate a company. Researching a business to buy takes time and focuses on discovering the truth about the enterprise being considered.

Buying a Franchise

Many small business owners have minimized their risks by investing in a franchise. Franchising is a plan of distribution where an individually-owned business is operated as a part of a large chain. The products and services offered are standardized. The company (franchisor) gives the individual dealer (franchisee) the right to market the franchisor's product or service and to use the franchisor's trade name, trademarks, reputation, and way of doing business. The franchise agreement usually gives the franchisee the exclusive right to sell in a specified area. In return, the franchisee agrees to pay to the franchisor a fee and/or a percentage of gross sales.

You may wish to explore the advantages of this means of business ownership. You will be able to start your business under a name and trademark that is already accepted by the public. You may be able to receive training and management assistance from people who are experienced in your type of business. You may also be able to obtain financial assistance from the franchisor. Often, equipment and supplies must be purchased from the franchisor. You could receive savings through the franchisor's quantity purchasing of products, equipment, supplies, and advertising materials. Some franchisors will guide you in day-to-day operations until you are proficient. Often, the franchisor provides management consulting on a continuing basis. This usually includes help with recordkeeping. National and regional promotions by the franchisor will help your business. The immediate identification many franchise operations enjoy can bring pre-sold customers to your door.

Promotion: the communication of information by a seller to influence the attitudes and behavior of potential buyers.

You should also look at some of the disadvantages. Because of the required standardized operations, you cannot make all of the rules. You often lose the freedom to be your own boss and to make most of the decisions. The franchisor usually charges a royalty on a percentage of gross sales and that royalty fee must ultimately come out of your profits. On the other hand, the franchisor does not usually share your losses. You may be restricted in establishing selling prices, in introducing new products or services, and in dropping unprofitable ones thus limiting your ability to be competitive. Franchisors require specific reports and you may consider the time and effort spent in preparing them to be burdensome. A **Buying a Franchise Worksheet** has been included on pages 18–19 to help you evaluate this type of business.

Making the decision to franchise is not a matter to take lightly. Before entering into a franchise contract do the following:

◈ *Examine your interests and abilities.* What do you like to do? What are you good at?

◈ *Consult a directory of franchise opportunities.* A number of organizations publish information that includes descriptions of franchisor companies and the qualifications and capital that a franchisee needs.

◈ *Narrow your options.* Write to the companies that interest you and ask them to give you the names of franchisees you can contact.

◈ *Talk to franchisees.* Other franchisees have firsthand experience at operating the type of business that interests you.

◈ *Contact the Federal Trade Commission.* The FTC can provide free information on the FTC Franchise Rule, which requires franchisors to disclose certain information before a potential franchisee invests any money in the opportunity. For an information packet, write to the Division of Marketing Practices, FTC, Washington, DC 20580 or call (202) 326-2258, or access the agency's Web site: www.ftc.gov.

◈ *Consult a lawyer and an accountant before signing a franchise contract.* Make sure that you understand all of the details and ramifications of the contract. Their terms usually last 10 to 20 years.

Contract: An agreement regarding mutual responsibilities between two or more parties.

You can prepare yourself to be successful by identifying all of the activities necessary for the development of your business. Then plan for each task to be handled properly. You can increase your chances of success by developing a business plan. A business plan serves as the foundation for

TECH TIP 3
Franchise Reports

FRANCHISE FAX is a service of FRANDATA Corporation and offers free reports on the franchise industry. Call 1-800-535-9399 from your fax machine, enter your fax number and follow the instructions to access the main menu. This will give you a list of the Industry Menus. For example, if you are interested in learning about computer product franchises, you would request Industry Menu #113. New reports are added regularly.

any new business. It is the blueprint for your business start-up, operation, and growth. Whether you are starting your own business, buying an existing business or buying a franchise, a business plan will help you make sound decisions for getting your business running and keeping it on track. Chapter 20 deals with this subject. For more comprehensive information, we have written a book entitled *Anatomy of a Business Plan* (Chicago: Dearborn, 1999) and developed companion software, *Automate Your Business Plan.*

Stepping Along

Now that you have decided on a type of business and a method for start-up, it is time to take the next step: researching your business idea to determine its profit potential. We do this by identifying and analyzing a **target market**. This refers to your customers or clients, the entities that will be paying their hard-earned money for your products and services. The mission of Chapter 3 is to show you how to determine how much your target market spends on your type of product or service, how much of that revenue has been captured by your competition, and what portion of that revenue will be yours.

Target market: the specific individuals, distinguished by socio-economic, demographic, and interest characteristics, who are the most likely potential customers for the goods and services of a business.

Buying a Business Worksheet

Name of business: _____ The Baseball Sports Shop _____

Type of business: _____ Retail store: Baseball equipment, uniforms, trading cards _____

Address: _____ 786 Cherry Lane, Blair, NY 18760 _____

_____

Contact person: _____ Sam and Alice Brockton, 555-0601 _____

Why is this business for sale? _____ Owner is retiring. _____

What is the history of this business? _____ Started in October 1976. Expanded and moved _____
to present location in June 1986. _____

Has this business been profitable? _____

_____ 1998 net profit = $86,000 _____

_____ 1999 net profit = $110,000 _____

_____ Profit increase due to addition of school uniform accounts. _____

_____

What will I be buying? _____

Accounts payable/liabilities: _____ $54,000 _____

Accounts receivable: _____ $21,000 (age of receivables) _____

Business name: _____ Name limits business to sale of baseball-focused items. _____
_____ Not an asset—will have to be changed. _____

Customer list: _____ 12,000 names—active customer list _____

Fixed assets: _____ $128,000 (Itemize balance sheet and note age and condition.) _____

Inventory: _____ $87,000 _____

Lease: _____ 2 years remaining on existing lease. Rent = $1,000/month _____

Personnel: _____ Must agree to keep current employees. 3 full-time sales clerks _____
_____ ($8/hr each). One bookkeeper ($25/hr). 6 part-time employees ($7/hr). _____

Proprietary rights (copyright, patent, trademark): _____ Trademark — logo. High school _____
_____ and university baseball uniform account = $70,000/yr. income. _____

Unpaid taxes: _____ Accrued $10,000 _____

What is the selling price of this business? _____ $240,000 _____

How will I finance this purchase? _____ Present owner will assist in financing. $80,000 _____
_____ down-payment. $160,000 financed at 8% over 25 years. _____

Buying a Franchise Worksheet

Name of franchise: American Sports and Trophies

Type of business: Retail store featuring full line of baseball, football, tennis equipment, footwear, clothing and trophy and engraving sales.

Address: 762 Industrial Parkway, Atlanta, GA 30601

Contact person: Al Casey (401) 555-6250

What is the reputation of the franchisor?   Well-established (1984)
     Good response from other franchisees interviewed.

Is the company involved in litigation?   None

What is the reputation of the individual business?
     Name recognition and public awareness are good.

What training and start-up assistance is offered by the franchisor?
     Six weeks management training in Atlanta—cost included in franchise fee.

What continuing assistance is offered by the franchisor?
     Location assistance, inventory control system, bookkeeping system, promotion and advertising assistance.

What is the management structure of the organization?
     Regional manager—Tom Anderson
     District manager—Ann Johnstone

Is the location and territory protected?
     6 mile radius protected

Buying a Franchise Worksheet, continued

What are the operating practices of the franchise? _____

Product line selected by franchisor.

Pricing structure determined by franchisor.

What are the operating control policies? _____

Quarterly financial reports

Co-op advertising costs

What are the franchise costs? _$280,000_

Initial license fee: _$100,000_

Continuing royalty fees: _2% of gross sales annually_

Other fees: _Equipment—$60,000_

Opening inventory—$120,000 (must be purchased from company)

How will the sale be financed? _Through franchisor_

Do I have the right to sell the franchise? _Must be sold through franchisor._

What are the terms of renewal and termination? _Contract written from year to year._

"Escape clause" favors franchisor

1. Non-renewal by franchisor if sales do not reach projections in agreement.

"Buy back clause"

1. Franchisor can repurchase franchise at will.

Determining Business Feasibility

Before officially starting a business, it is prudent to conduct a feasibility study. The word feasible is defined as that which is able to be done, that which is practical. In business, this is synonymous with profitable. Are there customers out there who are interested in what you are going to provide? Will they buy enough to support your financial obligations? Will your business idea cover your personal expenses as well as business expenses with enough revenue left over to allow for growth? The only way to determine this is to get the answers to a few simple questions and then analyze how these answers apply to your business idea.

◆ ◆ ◆ ◆ ◆

Your product or service may be in demand and your pricing competitive. You may have found the lowest prices for your raw materials and may have secured adequate financing for your business. All of this will be of no use if you have not taken the time to identify your customers and found the means to get your product or service to them. The key word here is **time**. It takes time to research a business idea, but it is time well spent. It may mean the difference between success and failure. Find out now if there is a need for your product or service **before** committing a great deal of time and money to the project.

Generating a Viable Business Idea

If you haven't yet decided on a business idea, you should reflect on your past experiences. Is there a particular hobby you enjoy? Do you have a unique knowledge? Has some experience such as travel or sports given you an expert perspective on a subject?

Do you have a passion for something—perhaps children, the elderly, reading, a social or political cause? Have you spent a number of years in a certain industry or doing a specific job function? Do you have a special skill or talent?

Sometimes it is helpful to get feedback from people who know you well. Ask them about your strengths and weaknesses. Brainstorm business ideas that seem to fit with your background and interests. It's important that your business idea is something you will know and enjoy. After all, you will be spending an awful lot of time researching your potential competitors, getting to know your customers, writing a business plan, and running your business. You had better well enjoy it!

Researching Your Market

Market research involves finding out what a customer wants and needs and determining how your business can satisfy those wants and needs. You will need to examine your competition's abilities and successes in the marketplace. Based on your research, you will project revenue—the amount of money that will flow into your business, and expenses—the amount of money you will spend. Try to be objective and think like a customer.

Viable: a business that is capable of earning enough revenue to sustain itself; to pay all of its expenses, pay its owner's salary, and have enough left to continue its growth.

There is a wealth of information available that will help you decide if your idea is viable. Begin by collecting data that applies to your business. There are two types of information you will need to collect. Start by observing the general environment and analyzing trends. This is often referred to as secondary data. Once you have examined the general environment, you will want to solidify this research by getting personal feedback, or primary data. At this stage you will talk directly with people who have the characteristics of your secondary data.

There are professional firms and individual consultants who can conduct market research for you. They conduct research on the general environment, produce market surveys, compile data, and make recommendations. This may be too costly for a small start-up business. You may choose to do your own work. The advantage of doing your own market research is that you will have firsthand knowledge of your industry and of your customers.

You will also want to examine trends that are prevalent in the marketplace you intend to serve. This may be global through e-commerce, regional in the form of transportable services such as mobile accounting agencies, or local as with corporate-sponsored, on-site childcare. Some current marketplace trends are:

◆ ***Technology.*** Recent technological innovations allow us to reach markets faster and easier than ever. E-commerce allows us to purchase products and services over the Internet. Pagers and cell phones provide instant communication. Office equipment such as fax machines, copiers, and voice mail systems are commonplace. Teleconferencing allows us to conduct meetings without leaving our respective offices. All of these new techniques need explanation and this new equipment needs service and repair.

◆ ***Fast action.*** Because of recent technological advances, we have gotten used to getting what we want in a very short amount of time. We can drive through fast food establishments; businesses are becoming mobile to bring their services directly to the consumer; and movies pack a lifetime of action into two hours! Will this change the way you will deliver your product or service to your customers?

◆ ***International commerce.*** Travel and language are no longer barriers to commerce. International trade has opened up wonderful opportunities for small business.

◆ ***Growing senior market.*** With an increase in the number of people age 65 and over, new opportunities are opening up for businesses in the area of health care, travel, and housing. The Bureau of Labor Statistics Consumer Expenditure Survey indicates that the 55 to 64 age group spends more on "toys, games, and hobbies" than any other group.

What is the climate for the business you want to start? Look for specific trends in your industry. Contact trade and professional associations in your field to determine the demand for the product or service you are considering. These entities can provide information on current acceptable pricing levels and average revenue by category.

For example, if you are interested in developing a hobby into a business, you will want to contact Hobby Industry Association (www.hobby.org). HIA conducts a biannual industry survey and can provide specific information regarding household spending patterns and average expenditures by craft category.

Link Resources has estimated that during the year 2000, 50 percent of all homes will contain an office. This may represent the full- and part-time self-employed or telecommuters who are employed by other companies but work from home. Perhaps you have a background in computer technology and love mechanical and assembly type work. You want to cash in on this growing market. Your local Business License Department can tell you how many home-based business licenses have been issued in your geographical area. What percentage of the population does the number represent? Has this number increased over the past five years?

Telecommute: Transmit work via a computer modem link from one office site to another.

Your chamber of commerce or Economic Development Department can provide population projections for your area.

If your business idea looks like it has possibilities at this point, look at the customer base for your business. Who is going to buy your product, who will use your service, how much are they going to spend, and how often do they make a purchase?

Finding Your Target Market

The goal of market research is to find your best customers. Target markets are those individuals or groups most likely to become your customers. They have common characteristics and needs that your business will be able to satisfy. Your goal is to develop a profile of your customers. Gather this information through the study of demographics and psychographics.

The word **demographics** refers to statistical information such as age, sex, ethnic background, education, occupation, income, family status, and geographic location.

> **Target market**: specific individuals or businesses, that based on socioeconomic, demographic, geographic, and interest/need considerations, are the most likely potential customers for the products and/or services of a business.

> **Demographics**: the statistical study of populations with reference to size, density, distribution, and vital statistics.

- ◈ *Population distribution* is one of several factors you will use to help you determine the size and location of the market. Studies show trends such as the shift of more affluent city dwellers to suburban communities.

- ◈ *Age distribution* dictates trends. The number of people age 65 and over is increasing, leading to a growing senior market.

- ◈ *Sex* is an obvious basis for consumer market analysis. Many traditional buying patterns are changing. The business example, Ace Sporting Goods, must not assume only men will be interested in fly-fishing!

- ◈ *Ethnic origin* may indicate product preferences, age distribution, population shifts, and language differences.

- ◈ *Family status* has changed in the past decade. Two distinct and new groups have emerged: single people living alone and unmarried people living together. If you are developing a take-out food business, look closely at the family status in your area. Will you be providing family-style meals or individual servings?

- ◈ *Education level, occupation, and income* are other demographics to be considered. Education level often points to changes in product preference. People with higher levels of education may have more specialized tastes and higher incomes. Occupation must also be considered as a meaningful criterion for analyzing the market.

Markets are also defined in terms of **psychographics**. These are psychological characteristics of your market and are as important as demographics. In fact, they often give insight into why people buy certain products or use certain services. The study of psychographics looks at lifestyle, personal behavior, self-concept, and buying style.

Psychographics: the system of explaining market behavior in terms of attitudes and life styles.

- *Lifestyle* refers to a person's manner of living. It is a broad category and involves personality characteristics. Lifestyle relates to a customer's activities, interests, and opinions. It reflects how leisure time is spent.

- *Personal behavior* is tied to personal values. The degree of community involvement, political activity, and neighborhood participation reflects the psychological makeup of a person. The degree of cautiousness, skepticism, and ambition reflects on buying patterns.

- *Self-concept* refers to how we see ourselves and hope to be seen by others. The demographics of family size, location, occupation, and income level may indicate an individual would purchase a minivan, but the psychographics of self-image show that the individual would buy a sports car.

- *Buying style* of your market is critical. How often do they make a purchase? Was there a specific reason for the purchase or was it an impulse buy? New products are first purchased by individuals who perceive themselves as adventuresome and open-minded.

Lifestyle: a pattern of living that comprises an individual's activities, interests, and opinions.

Collecting General (or Secondary) Data

Marketing information comes to us from many sources. Depending on the type of information you are seeking, you can access reports published by federal, state, and local governments, business directories, independent market research firms, associations, and the census. You might also consider media kits from radio, television, newspapers and magazines, and articles in magazines and trade journals. The list goes on.

Media kits: radio/television station and newspaper/magazine advertising department promotional packets.

Competition

Direct competition will be a business offering the same product or service to the same market through the same sales channels. **Indirect competition** is a company with the same product or service delivered to the market through different sales channels. For example, an independent bookstore will find direct competition from other bookstores in the geographical area they serve. They will find indirect competition from e-commerce entities such as Amazon.com, catalogs specializing in books, non-traditional booksellers such as grocery stores, and gift

Sales channels: the route a product follows as it moves from the original grower, producer, or importer to the ultimate consumer.

TECH TIP 4
Using the Internet to Research Your Market

You will do yourself a great service by using the Internet to conduct your research. It doesn't matter whether or not you own a computer, have Internet access, or are comfortable delving into this new, world-wide territory. You need to learn and there are ways to get help. Much of the information you will need can be found in your public or college library, and many libraries are now online. If a library in your area offers Internet access, set up an appointment to sit down at the terminal with a library staff member familiar with business reference sites who will help you find what you need. Another option is to visit your nearest SBA Business Information Center (BIC). There are centers located around the country that provide publications, use of computers, and often, Internet access. The SBA BIC Web address is www.sba.gov/gopher/Local-Information/Business-Information-Centers/Bics/.

A few Internet resources to get you started are as follows:

- Use your powers of observation and look around to see how you can capitalize on current buying and lifestyle trends. The Bureau of Labor Statistics has two Consumer Expenditure Surveys online. The surveys provide information on the buying habits of American Consumers, including data on their expenditures, income, and family characteristics. The site can be accessed at www.bls.gov/csxhome.htm.

- The Bureau of Economic Analysis, an agency of the U.S. Department of Commerce, is the nation's economic accountant. The BEA prepares estimates that highlight key national, international, and regional aspects of the U.S. economy. Their Web site, www.bea.doc.gov/, offers information on gross domestic product, industry and wealth data, and related articles.

- Trade and professional associations exist for every type of enterprise. Many have Web sites that detail their services and usually include "how to start a..." information. Gateway to Associations Online is a clearinghouse of hundreds of associations. To run a search, access their site at www.asaenet.org/gateway/onlineassocslist.html.

- Search engines are useful ways to obtain information. You simply plug in a word or phrase and the engine will see if there is anything listed under those key words. You will soon find that you will likely need to narrow your search if you are going to get any good information in a timely manner. Be specific.

AltaVista:	www.altavista.com
Hotbot:	www.hotbot.com
Infoseek:	www.infoseek.com
Lycos:	www.lycos.com
Yahoo:	www.yahoo.com

shops. Keep your eyes and ears open when identifying who your competitors are and where they are coming from.

Competition can be identified in a number of ways. Look through the business listings in your telephone directory to get an idea of the scope and location of the competition. The chamber of commerce and Economic Development Centers can provide information on business in general and your business area in particular for the region you wish to investigate. Your questionnaires and surveys may have indicated what companies your target market is currently using. Check to see if they belong to trade and professional associations.

Make a list of your competitors and a list of questions you want answered. Plan to visit each competitor and gather your data. Look at their pricing structure. Figure out their share of the total market. You may develop your own evaluation form or make copies of the **Competition Evaluation Form** on page 36. Complete one for each competitor.

When you analyze your evaluations, look for strengths and weaknesses in your competition. You will bring the strengths of the competition to your business and you will learn from their weaknesses. The weaknesses are your inroads to success. They point the way toward what will be **unique** about your business. They will help you identify what will **benefit your customer**. This information helps you capture your share of the market and may help you take some of the market away from your competitors.

Collecting Personal (or Primary) Data

After you have developed your idea, examined the trends for your business, and researched the competition and the general market environment, you will want to look more closely at how this information relates to the profitability of your business. Study the nature of the demand. Are your products or services seasonal? Are the products you provide and the services you offer a fad? Is there room for growth? Can you think of related products or services to round out your line?

You will want to talk to people firsthand about how your product or service solves a problem for them. Remember—this is essentially what your business will do for your customer. Now that you have researched your market, you will have a good idea of where to find them.

If your secondary research indicates that your target market is people in home-based businesses, is there an association representing home-based businesses where you can meet with owners, survey them, and determine their needs? At local office supply and furniture stores, have you noticed an increase in floor space devoted to modular, build-it-yourself computer consoles, and office furniture? Ask the manager how this market is changing. Do buyers need assistance in assembling these kits and in setting up their computers? Does the store provide this service and, if so, how much do they charge? How often are they called on to assemble office furniture? Do they set up computers in home offices? Observation and questioning can give you facts regarding demand for and interest in what you are proposing.

Trade show: industry and professional conferences where new products are introduced and showcased.

You may consider attending a trade show or conference that attracts your potential customers. Your attendance at trade shows will also introduce you to new products and services, give you indications of consumer demand, and allow you to meet with suppliers and vendors. Suppliers and vendors are also a rich source of information.

You might consider test marketing some samples of your product or providing your service free in exchange for critique and a possible testimonial letter. Don't use friends or relatives; their opinions generally aren't objective! Perhaps you could contact the chamber of commerce or another civic group to see if you could present samples at one of their meetings.

Use of Questionnaires

The most-used and most cost-effective method of gathering information on your target market is through the use of questionnaires. Surveys are an excellent means of determining the response to what you have to offer and a questionnaire is the most common means of collecting data. Contact the business departments of colleges and universities in your area. Students majoring in marketing may be required to conduct a market study and your business could fill that need. Your questionnaire results can form a basis for zeroing in on your customers. They can give you feedback regarding the demographics and psychographics of your study group. Be sure that you include questions that will generate the information you need.

Reach your market by giving the questionnaire to valid, potential customers, not family and friends. Your questionnaire should be circulated to people who meet the general characteristics you discovered in your secondary research. Surveying people who already have an interest in your product or service will greatly increase the validity of your survey. For example, Ace Sporting Goods is thinking of offering fly-fishing classes and fishing trips. It would be best to distribute the questionnaire in areas where people may have that interest, such as parks and preserves, sporting goods shows, sport associations, and outdoor clubs.

Your market can be contacted through the mail, by telephone, via e-mail, or through focus groups. You may rent a mailing list, use a geographical phone directory, or conduct interviews through clubs and organizations. Display tables at community events are also a good way to make contact with the buying public and gather information.

Plan your strategy for evaluation while you are developing your questionnaire. Use an **address code** on all of your mailings. For example, if your mailing address is 216 Main Street, code your return address by adding Suite 206 or Dept. 300. Suite 206 could be the code for mailings sent to a specific area. If the questionnaires are returned unsigned, you will still be able to have an idea of the geographical area responding. Department 300 could refer to a mailing sent in March of the year 2000. You also can color code your mailings. Print your questionnaires on different colors or different types of paper. Again, you will have a clear picture of the response from a geographical area.

A questionnaire begins with an introductory paragraph that must capture the readers interest. "I am interested in offering fly-fishing classes and fishing trips and want to be sure that I meet your needs." Get the reader to buy into your business concept; make them feel like a "partner" in this endeavor. They are much more likely to continue reading and to complete and return the survey if they feel their input will be valued.

A well-designed questionnaire can gather data covering four main areas:

1. *Interest in your product or service.* Include questions aimed at determining a need for your product or service. Would you be interested in home delivery of gourmet meals? How often would you use this service? How much do you spend in a month on take-out food?

2. *Demographics.* Questions can be structured to show you the kind of people your prospects are. These questions gather the demographic and psychographic information on your market. What is your age range? Do you work away from your home city? Do you shop where you work? Do you shop where you live? What price would you expect to pay for this product? What would you expect to pay for this service?

3. *The means for reaching your market.* Questions can be included that will show you how to reach your customers. What newspapers do you read? What radio stations do you listen to? What TV programs do you watch? Do you use discount coupons? Do you order through catalogs? Do you have an e-mail address? Do you shop over the Internet? Where would you expect to buy this product?

4. *The competition.* Questions about the competition can show you ways in which your company can be unique and can benefit the customer. What company do you currently use? What do you like about their product or service? How can the product or service be improved?

To illustrate how specific data can be gathered, a **Questionnaire Format Worksheet for Ace Sporting Goods** has been included on page 32. The business owner is interested in offering fly-fishing classes and guided fishing trips. Note the questions dealing with potential revenue: Would you be interested in classes on fly-fishing? Would you be interested in fishing trips? How much would you expect to pay for a ten-hour, guided fishing trip? The owner wants to know if the perceived target market is interested, how often they would use the service, and how much they would pay.

To help you develop your own survey, a **Sample Questionnaire for a Product** and a **Sample Questionnaire for a Service** have been included on pages 33–34.

To help you with your evaluation, we have included a **Questionnaire Coding Log** on page 35. Note the interest shown by Ace Sporting Goods' target market by groups, dates, and locations. Questionnaires can gather great information about where your market is located and how to reach them.

Identification of the total market and how much it spends is not enough. What percent of the total market has been already been captured by the competition?

Putting it Together

The key to market research is gathering useful information; information that is timely and reliable. It is an orderly, objective way of learning about the people who will buy your product or use your service. A **Target Market Worksheet** has been included on pages 37–38 for your use in defining your market. Notice how Ace Sporting Goods has condensed the information gathered through use of questionnaires, interviews, and mailing lists to get a composite of the customer base.

A **Market Research Worksheet** has been included on page 39 to show you how you can translate the results of your research into a plan for action. Analysis of the findings in term of potential revenue is included at the bottom of the example.

Remember that marketing is a dynamic process. Customers move, lifestyles change, income levels vary. To work effectively, market research must occur continuously throughout the lifetime of your business. Always be alert for new competition, new products and services, population shifts, and new trends. The process of researching, reaching, and retaining your target market is detailed in our book entitled *Target Marketing* (Chicago: Dearborn, 1996).

Stepping Along

At this point, it is a good idea to skip forward and read Chapter 17, "Success or Failure: It Depends on Your Cash Flow" before returning to work on Chapter 4. Don't be discouraged if some of the material or terms seem

Customer base: core group of customers or clients that a business relies upon and that fits a given profile.

foreign to you. By using this book you will gain the knowledge you need to understand an implement the material presented. It is always good to have a knowledge of where you are headed in terms of financial analysis. This will help you know what questions need to be asked as you move into the proceeding chapters. As you identify projected revenue from the sales of your product and/or service, refer to the **Sources of Cash Worksheet** on page 167 and the **Cash Flow Statement** on page 173. Begin filling in the blanks under "Cash Receipts." The next chapters of this book will assist you in determining your expenses. When the Cash Flow Statement has been completed, you will have a clear picture of not only how much money will be flowing into and out of your business, but when. You will be able to see the feasibility or profitability of your business and will be able to calculate your break-even point.

Questionnaire Format Worksheet
for Ace Sporting Goods

Date: _____ Location: _____

(Demographic and psychographic information)

Please circle answers:

Sex/status: Male   Female   Single   Married   Other

Age: 18 to 25   26 to 35   36 to 45   46 and over

Your Occupation/profession: _____

Do you enjoy outdoor activities? Yes_____ No_____

Do you enjoy fishing? Yes_____ No_____

(Information to determine interest and to learn about the competition)

Have you ever been fly-fishing? Yes_____ No_____

If yes:

    a) What did you think of the experience? _____

    b) Where did you go?   _____

    c) Were instructors/guides present? _____

    d) Would you be interested in classes on fly-fishing? _____

    e) Would you be interested in fishing trips? _____

    f) How much would you expect to pay for a 10-hour, guided fishing trip? _____

If no:

    a) Would you be interested in fishing lessons? _____

    b) Would you be interested in rental equipment? _____

    c) Would you be interested in free viewing of instructional sports videos in our store? _____

(Information on reaching the potential market)

Do you use discount coupons? Yes_____ No_____

What newspapers do you read?   _____

What radio station do you listen to? _____

Have you heard of Ace Sporting Goods? Yes_____ No_____

Thank you for your response. The following information is helpful to my study, but is optional:

Name: _____

Address: _____

City/State/Zip: _____

Phone: _____

Sample Questionnaire: Product

I am developing a new product and am contacting a few people in your neighborhood for an important and quick survey. I hope you will take a moment to tell me how you feel about board games.

1. Do you play any board games? Yes_____ No_____ (If no, please go to #7)

2. What is your favorite board game?

   Backgammon _____   Checkers _____   Pictionary® _____   Life® _____

   Clue® _____   Monopoly® _____   Sorry® _____   Other _____

3. On the average, how often do you play board games?

   Less than once per month _____   Once per month _____

   Twice per month _____   Once per week _____   More than once per week _____

4. Would you consider playing a new board game about the stock market?

   Yes_____   No_____   Maybe_____   I don't know_____

5. How much would you pay for a board game about the stock market?

   $6.00 to $10.00 _____ $10.01 to $15.00 _____ $15.01 to $20.00 _____   Over $20.00 _____

6. What is the first word that comes to mind when you think of the stock market? _____
   _____

7. On the average, how many hours of television do you watch per week?

   Less than one hour _____   1 to 3 hours _____   3 to 6 hours _____

   6 to 9 hours _____   9 hours or more _____

8. Do you clip coupons from the newspaper? Yes_____ No_____

9. What radio station do you listen to most often? _____

10. What is your age group?

    18 to 24 years _____   25 to 34 years _____   35 to 44 years _____

    45 to 54 years _____   Over 55 years _____

11. What is your average household income?

    Under $25,000 _____ $25,000 to $45,000 _____ $45,000 to $60,000 _____   Over $60,000 _____

Thank you for your response. The following information is helpful to my study, but is optional:

Name: _____

Address: _____

City/State/Zip: _____

Phone: _____

Sample Questionnaire: Service

I am developing a new product and am contacting a few people in your neighborhood for an important and quick survey. I hope you will take a moment to tell me how you feel about take-out food.

1. Do you order take-out food? Yes_____ No_____

2. What is your favorite take-out food?

   Pizza _____   Deli food _____   Mexican food _____

   Burgers _____   Chinese food _____   Other _____

3. On the average, how often do you order take-out food?

   Less than once a month _____   Once a month _____

   Twice a month _____   Once a week _____   More than once a week _____

4. Would you consider full course take-out meals?   Yes_____   No_____

5. Would you consider home-delivered meals?   Yes_____   No_____

6. How much would you be willing to pay for a full course, home-delivered meal?

   $10.00 _____ $15.00 _____ $17.50 _____ $20.00 _____

7. What is the first word that comes into your mind when you think of full course, home-delivered

   meals? _____

8. On a scale of one to five, with five signifying very important, please rank the following items as they relate to your feelings about take-out food: *(please circle)*

Containers	1	2	3	4	5
Combinations of foods offered	1	2	3	4	5
Temperature when delivered	1	2	3	4	5
Taste	1	2	3	4	5
Delivery time	1	2	3	4	5

9. Do you clip coupons from the newspaper? Yes_____ No_____

10. What newspaper do you read? _____

11. What is your age group?

   18 to 24 years _____   25 to 34 years _____   35 to 44 years _____

   45 to 54 years _____   Over 55 years _____

12. What is your average household income?

   Under $25,000 _____ $25,000 to $45,000 _____ $45,000 to $60,000 _____   Over $60,000 _____

Thank you for your response. The following information is helpful to my study, but is optional:

Name: _____

Address: _____

City/State/Zip: _____

Phone: _____

Questionnaire Coding Log
for Ace Sporting Goods

Code	Date	Number Sent	Destination/ Recipient	Response Rate	Evaluation
Blue paper	9/00	500	Wed. 10 AM to 1 PM Shoppers at Fisherman's Wharf Mall	20 interviews 36 returned by mail	6 follow-up for classes/trips 30 follow-up
Yellow paper	9/00	500	Sat. 10 AM to 1 PM Shoppers at Fisherman's Wharf Mall	52 interviews 160 returned by mail	20 follow-up for classes/ trips 52 follow-up
Dept. 900	9/00	1000	Mailing list #132 18-35 yrs. Live in 10 mile radius $35,000 average income	10/00 120 returned	26 follow-up for classes/ trips
Suite 900	9/00	500	Mailing list—local university students	10/00 287 returned	158 follow-up for classes/ trips
Dept 1000	10/00	1000	Mailing list #132 repeat rental	11/00 261 returned	57 follow-up for classes/ trips

By analyzing the questionnaire results, the owner of Ace Sporting Goods can determine that the Saturday shoppers at the Fisherman's Wharf Mall are more responsive. The questionnaire can be analyzed to get a composite of demographic information. The mailing to university students got a good response and this group will likely form a good part of the target market. The response to the 9/00 and 10/00 mailings indicates the value of repeat mailings to the same group. Through the mailings, the business owner has developed his own mailing list of names of 349 individuals interested in fishing trips and classes.

Competition Evaluation Form

1. Competitor: Smith Sporting Goods

2. Location: 724 University Drive, Blair, NY 07682

3. Products or services offered: Full line of sports equipment with emphasis on golf

4. Methods of distribution: Retail sales, catalog

5. Image: Blue and white colors used in decor and uniforms

   Packaging: Plastic sales bags with logo

   Promotional materials: Baseball caps and T-shirts with name and logo

   Methods of advertising: KLXY radio ads, flyers-mail, Sunday supplement-newspaper.

   Quality of product or service: Major brands, excellent sales staff

6. Pricing structure: 100% mark-up on golf items, 75% mark-up on other merchandise

7. Business history and current performance: In current location for five years

8. Market share (number, types, and location of customers):   One of two sporting goods stores in town, has high school and university trade

9. Strengths (the strengths of the competition become your strengths):   Knowledgeable sales staff, established contacts with local golf courses and associations

10. Weaknesses (looking at the weaknesses of the competition can help you find ways of being unique and of benefiting the customer):

    - Does not offer classes or sports clinics

    - Closed Sundays

    - Does not stock fishing gear

    - Does not sponsor a youth team

Note: A Competition Evaluation Worksheet should be made for each competitor. Keep these records and update them. It pays to continue to rate your competition throughout the lifetime of your business.

Target Market Worksheet
for Ace Sporting Goods

1. Who are my customers?

   Profile: Results from questionnaires, interviews, mailing lists

   Economic level: 52% college graduates   25% management

   29% professionals   79% own or are buying homes

   Psychological make-up (lifestyle): Value reliability of merchandise (guarantee)

   Outgoing, athletic; like to travel

   Age range: Average age = 32

   Sex: Male = 57% Female = 43%

   Income level: Average household income = $58,000

   69% income from two wage earners

   Buying habits: Use coupons. Quality and reliability more important than cost.

2. Where are my customers located?

   Where do they live: Within city limits of Blair, NY

   Where do they work: 62% commute 20 to 35 miles, one way   24% work in Blair

   14% retired

   Where do they shop: 32% of the commuters shop where they work and arrive home

   after 6 PM

3. Projected size of the market:

   Target group represents 20% of total population within city limits.

   Total population = 52,000; 20% = 10,400

   Projections indicate that I can serve 10% of the targeted group for a

   customer base of 1040.

Target Market Worksheet, continued

4. What are the customers needs?

 a. Sports instruction. Opportunity to "try" equipment prior to purchase.

 b. Have interest in fishing, especially fly-fishing. Currently no store stocks a full product line of fishing gear.

 c. Due to commute time and number of two income families, store should be open at times convenient to the consumer.

 d. Business commitment to the community.

 e. Knowledgeable staff.

 f. Reliability of merchandise.

5. How can I meet those needs?

 a. Offer rental equipment. Offer sports clinics and classes. Offer "how-to" sports videos for in-store viewing. If demand is present, will add videos to product line.

 b. Stock full line of fishing gear. Provide in-store demonstration.

 c. Will open on Sunday. Will stay open until 9 PM on Thursday and Friday.

 d. Sponsor youth sports team.

 e. Training program for employees: sales techniques, customer service, sports knowledge.

 f. Offer in-store guarantee on all merchandise.

6. What is unique about my business?

 Only sporting goods store in the county to stock and specialize in fishing equipment.

 Only store to provide an area for viewing sport instructional videos.

 In-store guarantee on all equipment.

Market Research Worksheet for Ace Sporting Goods

Questions	Information Source	Results	Effect on Plan
Would you be interested in fly-fishing lessons?	Mail list—27% response Questionnaire: Mall—Wednesday Mall—Saturday	241 interested 36 72	Expect 10% commitment or 35 class registrations. Offer one class Sat. 10 AM One class Wed. 10 AM
Would you be interested in guided fishing trips?	Mail list—27% response Questionnaire: Mall—Wednesday Mall—Saturday	241 interested 36 72	Expect 5% commitment or 17 class registrations. Offer one Sat. fishing trip limited to ten people.
How much would you expect to pay for a ten-hour fishing trip to the mountains?	Mail list—27% response Questionnaire: Mall—Wednesday Mall—Saturday	Average $65 (241 responded) avg. $45 avg. $55	Provide ten hr. guided trip to Carson River for $55/person. (average of all responses)
What is your age group?	Mail list response Questionnaire: Mall—Wednesday Mall—Saturday	majority 25–34 35–44 35–44	Most responses fall within 25–34 range—average age is 32. Will use this factor in future mail list rental.

The results of direct mail, telemarketing, questionnaires, and networking can be translated and put into action on the Market Research Worksheet. For example, 349 people indicated an interest in guided fishing trips. It is realistic to expect five percent or 17 people to actually register for the trip. The results indicate that $55 is the average amount registrants would expect to pay for a ten-hour guided fishing trip to the mountains. After considering salaries for two guides, rental of a 12-person van, insurance, fishing permits, and equipment, financial projections may indicate that the trip would have to include ten people at a charge of $60 per person in order to break even. If Ace Sporting Goods wants to make a profit, more people could be included and costs may be cut. The market has already indicated that they will not pay much over $55. The store may consider breaking even with the hope of generating future equipment sales. One trip could be scheduled to test the response. The Market Research Worksheet helps you to put into perspective the information you have gathered on your customers.

Choosing a Business Name

Now that you have decided what your business will be, you must choose your business name. If you purchase a franchise, that decision will be made for you. If you purchase an existing business, you may want to keep the same name or change to a new one. If you develop your own business, you will also have to develop a business name.

✦ ✦ ✦ ✦

The name you select explains who you are, identifies what sets you apart in the marketplace, and determines how you are perceived. This is an extremely important decision that takes careful consideration and research. Your business name is not something you will want to change; it will be your identification for many years. A name change can also be expensive; office supplies, marketing materials, signage, directory listings, and memberships are a few of the items that would have to be changed, if you change your business name.

Before deciding on your business name, consider the following factors:

✦ ***Choose a name that has meaning for your target market.*** Identify three to five personality traits or benefits that make your company special. These are the reasons for customers to decide to choose your business over that of the competition. Some examples are peace of mind, economy, friendliness, and innovation. Focus on the qualities your target customers appreciate. Make up a list of words or phrases that come to mind and are associated with the trait. Could this word be used as a business name? For example, the California high-tech company, Oracle, implies visionary power.

◆ *Avoid cute and clever names.* While unique names are usually easier to remember and may grab the attention of the consumer, the general rule is that they may not convey a business-like image. This would include names that play on words or have double meanings. Many wholesalers will not view the business as legitimate, even though you may be running a full-scale operation. Of course, there are exceptions to every rule. "Nice to Be Kneaded" is a good name for a massage center and "Franks for the Memory" is a memorable name for a snack bar featuring hot dogs! The bottom line is, will it attract buyers from your target market?

◆ *Use a descriptive name to advertise your product or service.* The consumer who sees your name will immediately associate it with the product or service you provide. For example, "Anderson's Financial Services," lets the consumer know the service being provided. "Anderson and Associates" does not. While conducting business, we all collect business cards. Later, when we look through the cards, we often haven't a clue as to the nature of a business if the name is not descriptive. Get some advertising mileage out of your business name.

◆ *Try not to have the name be restrictive.* Select a name that can become an umbrella for future products and services. If your business has been established to bring trendy products to the marketplace, avoid using a name that keys into a product with a short life span. It is better to give the business an umbrella name that covers a range of anticipated products and then choose a clever name for the individual products. Don't make your business name so specific that you cannot expand your business without the name losing its descriptive quality. It is not always easy to anticipate the directions your company may take, but try to project your future growth. It is difficult to change your business name once it is established. You risk losing the customer base and the goodwill you have built.

◆ *Think about how the name looks.* Sometimes a name becomes memorable because it can be paired with an effective visual image. For example, Apple Computer's logo is a rainbow apple with a bite taken out of it. Turtle Wax visually supports its name with the image of a hard-shelled turtle.

◆ *Plan for all uses of your business name.* Consider how your name could be abbreviated. Long names will not fit on computer generated mailing labels. If you are considering international trade, research the translation of your name into the languages of other countries.

Goodwill: the reputation generated by the conduct of you and your staff as well as the quality and performance of your product or service.

◆ *Consider alphabetical listings in directories.* It is to your advantage to be listed closer to the A's than to the Z's. You have a captive audience through your directory listings. Consumers and clients do not look through business and professional directories unless they are trying to locate products or services. They generally look through the first few listings when deciding who to call.

◆ *Check the white and Yellow pages of area phone directories.* Study how other businesses use the words you may be considering. Usually, there will be many businesses with names starting with your city's name, the name of a regional landmark, common terms such as "Quality." When business names begin to look generic, potential customers tend to overlook or forget them.

◆ *Use your own name.* If you are already well-respected in your community or field of business, you may want to use your own personal name as part of your business name. It may give you a head start in the business world. If you use your full legal name, you may not have to file a DBA ("Doing Business As," see Chapter 11). Some states require you to register if only your last name is used in the business name. If you have a common name, you may still wish to file the DBA for protection of the name in reference to your business. For example, if your name were Jane Smith, you might register "Jane Smith Contracting" because Jane Smith is a common name.

TECH TIP 5
Domain Name Choice, Usage, and Registration

When you create a Web site, use your business name as a domain name. You can get extra mileage out of your business name when you are able to also register it as your domain name.

For example, when Camille LeVasseur was developing Cal Consulting, her California-based computer consulting company, she registered the domain name calconsulting. Her internet address is www.calconsulting.com. Her e-mail address consists of her user name and her domain name; camille@calconsulting.com. You can see how this has made it easy for clients to reach her and has given added exposure to her business name.

Even though, at this time, you may not be planning to develop a Web site as part of your marketing strategy, you may want to research the availability of using your company name or brand identity in your domain name. The InterNIC (Internet Network Information Center) serves as an international registry for domain names so that duplicate names or addresses do not proliferate. To register your domain name, go to: www.internic.com.

Note: If you are thinking about using your own name, consider your long-range plan for the business. When you sell the company, you may also sell the business name…your name! The new owner may not conduct business in the same manner you do and you may risk losing your good name.

Narrowing the Search

At this point, you will have narrowed your list of potential names. Let the list rest for a few days. Then review it and delete names that do not fit the image of your business. Think about how you would react to the various names if you were a prospective client or customer. Share the list with family, friends, and associates. Ask which name best communicates what your business is about. Usually one name rises to the surface. Take your top three choices and check their availability.

Name Availability

Be sure the name you are considering for your business is available for use. There are a few horror stories about businesses who did not check their name's availability and later discovered the name legally belonged to someone else. To the best of your ability, determine that the name is not already in use. Check through the telephone directories in the public library. City and county business licensing offices can help you check for local use.

Trademark: a unique word, symbol, name, design, logo, slogan, or some combination of these used by a company to identify its product.

Trademarked names can be found in the Trademark Directories in State and Federal depositories and at many county and university libraries.

Each state has an office responsible for the registration of names of businesses incorporated within that state, out-of-state corporations qualified to do business in the state, and names that have been registered or reserved by other corporations. Generally this office falls under the jurisdiction of the Secretary of State. Even if you are not considering forming a corporation as your legal structure, it is to your advantage to use this resource in researching the availability of your business name. If you choose to incorporate later, you will want to use your current name as your corporate name since it will be associated with your product or service. Most often, name infringement does not become a problem until you become visible in the marketplace and create a threat to the business that feels it has prior claim to the name. The time you spend in researching name availability can end up being very cost-effective.

Infringement: use of a name or material that has been legally registered to another entity.

TECH TIP 6
Researching Business Name Availability

Another way to research name availability is to call up your favorite Web search engines and run a search. All search engines are not alike; an effective search requires at least a passing familiarity with your search engine's query language. Go to the site, click on the "help" button, and print out the information that tells you how to search it. Effectively used, a Web search can locate uses of the name you have chosen.

Two Internet Web sites that contain information on business name development and protection of that name through trademark are:

www.new-direction.com/name.htm

www.namestormers.com/nameg.htm

Many libraries and Small Business Development Centers provide access to the Internet which can assist you with a Trademark search and can enable you to conduct your research over a wide area. The U.S. Patent and Trademark site is:

www.uspto.gov

Note: Do not use the word "corporation" in your business name unless you have chosen and registered that form of legal structure. Smith Corporation may sound larger and more established than Smith Company, but unless the company is a legitimate corporation, the use of the term will be illegal.

Choosing a business name is a very personal decision and not one to be rushed into. Take time to choose a name that projects the image you desire for your company. Choose one that is memorable, available, and allows your company to move into the new millennium.

Corporation: a voluntary organization of persons, either actual individuals or legal entities, legally bound together to form a business enterprise.

Choosing a Business Location

Your choice of location should be made early on in your plans to start a business. The first thing to consider is whether the location you choose is right for your type of business. What has your study of demographics and your market identification shown you? Base your decision on the type of products and services you provide and your target market rather than on your personal convenience. Your most important consideration in choosing a location is your ability to satisfy your target market. Retail stores and restaurants have to be located where customers can reach them easily and safely. Service businesses such as exterminators and landscapers who go to a client's site can be more flexible in location choice. Manufacturers may find locations remote from the customer base to be the most cost-effective because of availability of raw materials, availability of labor, taxes, regulations, and overhead costs. You may have discovered that your market expects to order via fax or over the Internet. Make sure the site you choose is appropriate for your market.

❖ ❖ ❖ ❖ ❖

Location Evaluation

One of the most effective ways to evaluate a location is to do a map analysis. Draw a map of the area you wish to locate in. Have a copy shop run off some duplicates and one transparency. On the transparency, indicate the location sites available within your target area and mark them with a colored pen or assign each of them a number. You will be coding information onto the duplicate maps. You will be able to place the transparency over the coded map in order to get a feeling for each site. For instance, take one of the duplicate maps to the police department. Ask about crime rates. Shade the high crime area on your map. When you place the transparency over the shaded duplicate, you will be able to see if any of your potential locations fall within high crime areas.

Market.   On another duplicate map, shade in the areas where your target market lives, shops, or works. Again use the transparency overlay to see if your customers will be able to reach you easily. Retail stores and restaurants have to be located near their customers. Is there freeway access, good traffic flow, and adequate parking? Customers are concerned about safety. Can they reach your place of business with a feeling of security? Your crime rate map will show if they have to pass through any high crime areas on the way to your establishment. Customers' trips to your business should be pleasant. Drive and walk the routes your customers will have to take and get a feeling for the neighborhood.

Competition.   Find out where your competition is located and try to determine their sales volume. Most businesses try to distance themselves from the competition. However, some types of businesses, such as restaurants and auto dealerships, seem to have great success when clustered together. Professional services tend to locate within an area around a main support facility such as doctors' offices near a hospital and attorneys' offices near the court house. The consumer expects to find such services in these areas.

Sources of supply.   Manufacturing companies may need to locate close to suppliers and will have to consider the transportation, labor and power costs, the tax base, and the zoning regulations of a site. If certain raw materials are crucial to the manufacture of your products, you may need to locate close to your suppliers in order to reduce freight costs and delivery times.

Labor force.   Another location consideration is the availability of employees. As your business grows, it becomes increasingly important to have a pool of qualified potential employees. Some areas do not have an adequate group of people to form a labor pool. The prevailing wage rate in the area may be out of line with competitor's rates in other areas. The local chamber of commerce will be able to give you wage and labor statistics for the location you are considering.

Cost.   Office space for minimal rent is not always the best reason for choosing a site. There usually is a reason why the rent is low. Find out why the space is available, how long it has been vacant, and the history of the previous tenants. If there has been a frequent turnover in occupancy, it may be considered a "bad location." The chamber of commerce can give you information on average square footage costs for your area.

Volume: an amount or quantity of business; the volume of a business is the total it sells over a period of time.

Suppliers: individuals or businesses that provide resources needed by a company in order to produce goods and services.

Check with the local zoning commission regarding any rezoning being planned for the surrounding area. Take a walk around the area. Does the location project the image that you have for your business?

Before beginning a search for the perfect location, outline your present requirements and project your future needs. If you plan to grow your business, will the location allow for that expansion? It is often difficult to relocate a successful business without losing some of your customer base. A **Location Analysis Worksheet** has been included on pages 53–54 to help you evaluate the locations you will be considering.

Shopping Center

You may consider locating your business in a mini-mall or shopping center. These sites are preplanned as merchandising units. On-site parking is available, which makes it easy for your customer to drive in, park, and shop. You can take advantage of the foot traffic that is drawn to the area by other stores.

There may be some disadvantages, however. You will be a part of a merchant team. You will be expected to pay your share of the site budget, which may include items such as building, landscaping, parking lot maintenance, co-op advertising, and promotional activities. You may have to keep regular store hours, maintain your windows and premises in a prescribed manner, and conform to established display guidelines. In larger shopping centers, you may be required to pay a percentage of your gross sales to the developers or mall owners in addition to the rent or lease payments.

Look carefully at the history and health of anchor tenants in a shopping center setting. Few small businesses are themselves "destination locations." They must count on anchor tenants to draw traffic and the failure or relocation of the anchor tenant can have a serious impact on the small business.

Anchor tenant: a major or key company in a commercial area that acts as a destination location and attracts customers.

Business Incubators

A new entity has emerged in the location market: the business incubator. Business incubators are especially suited to light manufacturing and service businesses that do not require large facilities. To reduce overhead costs for new businesses, the incubator program offers a number of services to tenants through a centralized resource station. Usually included in the tenant package are receptionist services, telephone response and conference call capability, Internet access, maintenance of building and grounds, conference room facilities that may have teleconferencing capability, and access to shipping and receiving services such as UPS

Service business: a retail business that deals in activities for the benefit of others.

TECH TIP 7
Business Incubators

The National Business Incubator Association maintains a Web site that provides a clearinghouse for information on the business incubator industry. Links are provided to an Information Resource Center and to topical articles. The site can be accessed at: www.nbia.org/

Chamber of commerce: an organization of business people designed to advance the interests of its members. There are three levels: national, state, and local.

Lease: a long term rental agreement.

and FedEx. Other services may include complete clerical services at a nominal charge. Incubator facilities are targeted toward new and smaller companies and offer lower overhead costs during the start-up stage. Many sites can be industry-specific such as software development incubators or light manufacturing/assembly facilities. Contact your chamber of commerce, Economic Development Department, or local SBDC to identify incubators in your area.

Enterprise Zones

We have been hearing a great deal about the advantages of locating in enterprise zones as communities work toward redeveloping depressed areas. Companies located in these zones can take advantage of significant tax incentives and marketing programs. Enterprise zone communities are committed to attracting new business investment and offer such incentives as reduction or elimination of local permit and construction-related fees and faster processing of plans and permits. Information on enterprise zones in your area can be obtained through the Department of Commerce, the Small Business Administration, and the local chamber of commerce.

Lease Provisions

A lease is a binding legal agreement between a landlord (the lessor) and a tenant (the lessee). It details the rights and obligations of each party. Signing a lease is a serious financial transaction; before signing any lease agreement, have the document reviewed by an attorney or by a SCORE or SBDC consultant familiar with lease provisions. Following are some major considerations that must be understood and resolved to your satisfaction before a lease is signed:

Rent. How much is the rent payment and how is it computed? Various methods can be used to determine the amount to be paid.

1. Flat monthly payment which remains the same throughout the term of the lease.

2. Set percentage of your gross sales. Note that percentage is based on gross sales without consideration for your expenses, draw, etc.

3. Sliding percentage of your gross sales; the percentage varies at different increments of sales volume.

4. Combination of set minimum payment and a percentage of your gross sales.

Term.   How long will the lease be in effect? Do you have the option to renew?

Sublet.   Do you have the right to rent out unused space to another party? This could be valuable if you find that you have leased too much space. You may have a dry cleaning business and the addition of a tailor and/or an on-site shoe-repair facility would make you a one-stop-shop for your customers. Will your growth be limited by the terms of your lease?

Leasehold improvements.   Who is responsible for painting, remodeling, and other initial improvements? Who will pay for the improvements? Who will own the improvements, once made? Is the

---

 ## TECH TIP 8
Web-Based Information of Location and Lease Considerations

The Online Women's Business Center Web site contains a wealth of information covering all areas of business development and operation. Key categories entitled "Learning about Business," "Running a Business," "Information Exchange," and "Resources" provide access to numerous articles, references, discussion groups, and databases. The following Web address will lead you to an online article entitled "Choosing a Location for Your Business." Click on hot links within the text to be taken to additional information. Of special interest is the hot link, "lease negotiations," at the end of the article. This link will take you to additional information on analyzing lease costs and understanding lease terms. The site is reached at:

www.onlinewbc.org/docs/starting/location.html

Before signing a lease, make sure that you understand all of its terms and provisions. It is a good idea to have a lease for business property reviewed by a professional. Phone the Legal Referral Service listed in the yellow pages of your phone directory or access the following Web sites to locate a professional in your area to review your lease:

Service Corps of
Retired Executives (SCORE):   www.score.org

Small Business
Development Center (SBDC):   www.asbdc-us.org

building up to code? For example, the American with Disabilities Act requires that commercial, nonresidential property in which public goods or services are provided be free of all architectural barriers.

Insurance.   What insurance does the landlord provide? What coverage are you required to have? The landlord usually covers for accidents and damages that may occur in the common area. You may be required to have insurance to cover accidents, fire, theft, etc. in the leased area.

Security deposit.   Most landlords require a sum of money held during the term of the lease or occupancy to be used for any damage, lost rent, etc. This can be a sizable amount and must be included in your budget.

Termination.   Under what conditions does either party have a right to terminate the lease agreement?

Restrictions.   Are there any restrictions on the part of the landlord, the City, the Zoning Commission, or any agency regarding the use of the property?

Be sure you understand all of the provisions of the lease and that they fit with your plans for the site and for your business. Be sure to transfer information regarding security deposit, leasehold improvements, and rent to your Cash Flow Statement.

Location Analysis Worksheet
for Ace Sporting Goods

1. Address: _271 Adams Street, Blair, NY 07682_

2. Name, address, phone number of Realtor/contact person: _James Jones Century Realty,_
   622 Mason Street, Blair, NY 07682, 555-7093

3. Square footage/cost: _Retail shop space of 2,000 sq. ft. @$2.50/sq. ft., 50 ft. of_
   window display area fronting on high foot traffic area. Classroom area in back
   of store.

4. History of location: _Previous occupant: retail clothing outlet occupied site for seven_
   years. Moved to larger store. Site vacant for two months.

5. Location in relation to target market: _Primary retail and business sector for Blair._
   Draws customers from 20 mile radius.

6. Traffic patterns for customers: _Bus stop—1/2 block; easy access from First Avenue_
   and Main Street; traffic lights at crosswalks; customer merchandise pick-up area
   access in alley behind store.

7. Traffic patterns for suppliers: _Alley access for deliveries._

8. Availability of parking (include diagram): _Diagonal parking: 12 spaces in front of store;_
   parking lot one block away.

9. Crime rate for the area: _24-hour security in business sector; active neighborhood_
   watch in surrounding residential area.

10. Quality of public services (e.g., police, fire protection): _Police station: 6 blocks; fire_
    station: 2 miles; fire alarm, sprinkler system, smoke alarms in place.

11. Notes from walking tour of the area: _Homes well tended on north side; apartment_
    house 2 blocks south—two abandoned cars; debris piled in vacant lot—3 blocks
    east of site.

Location Analysis Worksheet, continued

12. Neighboring shops and local business climate: Dry cleaning/shoe repair; restaurant
    Good foot traffic; Association of Business Owners oversees the area.

13. Zoning regulations: Commercial

14. Adequacy of utilities (get information from utility company representatives):   6 phone lines into
    site; 2 bathrooms in store; city water, sewer. 220 wiring in place. No gas available.

15. Availability of raw materials/supplies: UPS, common carriers—daily delivery.

16. Availability of labor force: Temporary employment agency in business center.·
    University 5 miles away; high school 8 miles away

17. Labor rate of pay for the area: $5.50/hr. average for store sales people; $10.00/hr. for
    store manager; $7.00/hr. for instructors/guides

18. Housing availability for employees: Apartments and single family homes available in
    ten mile radius. Average rental for two bedroom = $450; average sale for two
    bedroom home = $86,000

19. Tax rates (state, county, income, payroll, special assessments):   State income tax = 7%;
    state sales tax = 6.5%

20. Evaluation of site in relation to competition: Smith Sporting Goods: Smith Sporting Goods:
    six miles away, has better parking, located closer to university and high school.
    This location is housed in a mini-mall and offers more adjacent businesses, has a
    lower square footage cost and has more foot traffic than the location of Smith
    Sporting Goods.

Developing a Home-Based Business

One of the fastest growing markets in the United States is the home-based business. It's interesting to note that one in five businesses located in an office or industrial area started in the home, including such well-known companies as Ford and Apple.

❖ ❖ ❖ ❖

It has been estimated that more than 24 million Americans are self-employed and working at home. This does not count those who were doing so on a part-time basis while holding a "regular" job. Part-time self-employed homeworkers numbered an additional 900,000.

Home-based businesses span a wide range of occupations and industries. One multi-state study of 900 home businesses and home workers conducted by a team of university-based researchers found that the top five occupations were marketing/sales (24%), contracting (15%), mechanical/transportation (13%), services (12%), and professional/technical (12%). Other studies yield varying results, but they all indicate that home businesses represent a wide range of occupations and industries.

The trend toward home-based business has occurred for several reasons. The advent of the electronic age with its computers, fax machines, modems, copiers, and other office technology has made it possible for almost every family to start a business from home. Job insecurities and layoffs have forced white-collar workers to pile out of corporations. Many of these displaced middle-management people have taken their skills home and translated them into viable businesses run from their home offices. The trend toward home-based business has also been impacted by economic considerations such as eliminating rent and utilizing other home-office deductions. As an additional bonus, having a home-based business has allowed parents to stay home with their families and addressed elder care and parental leave without added costs.

Home-based businesses can be very successful. They can also turn into disasters or, at the very least, unproductive attempts to run a business. In order to help you get off to a good start, this chapter contains some of the most important considerations that will contribute to the success of your home-based business.

Do You Qualify for a Home Office Deduction?

To qualify for a home office deduction for the business use of your home, you must use that portion of your home exclusively and regularly for your trade or business and it must be your principal place of business.

1. *Exclusive use.* To qualify under the exclusive use test, you must use a specific area of your home solely for your trade or business. The area used for business can be a room or other separately identifiable space. The space does not need to be marked off by a permanent partition. Exceptions apply if you use part of your home for the storage of inventory or product samples, or you use part of your home as a daycare facility.

2. *Regular use.* To qualify under the regular use test, you must use a specific area of your home for business on a continuing basis. You do not meet the test if your business use of the area is only occasional or incidental, even if you do not use that area for any other purpose.

3. *Trade or business use.* To qualify under the trade or business use test, you must use part of your home in connection with a trade or business. If you use your home for a profit-seeking activity that is not a trade or business, you cannot take a deduction for its business use.

4. *Principal place of business.* To qualify to deduct the expenses for the business use of your home, your home must be your principal place of business for that trade or business.

New 1999 Rules for Business Use of Your Home

New rules that went into effect beginning with the 1999 tax year have made it easier to claim a deduction for the business use of your home. Under the new rules, you may qualify to claim the deduction even if you never qualified before. **Note:** The information does not apply if you are filing under an extension for business use of your home in 1998.

Definition of Principal Place of Business for 1999

If you use your home exclusively and regularly for administrative or management activities of your trade or business and you have no other fixed location where you conduct substantial administrative or management activities of your trade or business, you can deduct expenses for your home office.

There are many activities that are administrative or managerial in nature. Some of these activities are:

◈ Billing customers, clients, or patients

◈ Keeping books and records

◈ Ordering supplies

◈ Setting up appointments

◈ Forwarding orders or writing reports

Administrative or management activities performed at other locations. Under the new rules, the following activities will not disqualify your home office as your principal place of business.

◈ You have others conduct your administrative or management activities at locations other than your home. (For example, another company does your billing from its place of business.)

◈ You conduct administrative or management activities at places that are not fixed locations of your business, such as in a car or a hotel room.

◈ You occasionally conduct minimal administrative or management activities at a fixed location outside your home.

◈ You conduct substantial non-administrative or non-management business activities at a fixed location outside your home. (For example, you meet with or provide services to customers, clients, or patients at a fixed location of the business outside your home.)

◈ You have suitable space to conduct administrative or management activities outside your home, but choose to use your home office for those activities instead.

Other Tests

These new rules for principal place of business will not affect the other tests you must meet to claim the expenses for the business use of your home. You still must use the business part of your home both exclusively and regularly for your trade or business. If you are an employee, the business use of your home must be for the convenience of your employer. In addition, your deduction may be limited if your gross income from the business use of your home is less than your total business expenses.

Calculating Your Deduction

To determine the deduction for the business use of your home, you have to find the percentage of the total area that is being used for business

TECH TIP 9

Download and Print IRS Publication 587: Business Use of Your Home

The Internal Revenue Service has a 27-page publication that will give you more comprehensive information on issues pertaining to the business use of your home. It addresses such things as: qualifying for a deduction, figuring deductions, deducting expenses, depreciating your home, daycare facilities, sale or exchange of your home, business furniture and equipment, recordkeeping, etc. It also contains worksheets that will help you figure your own deduction.

Publication 587: *Business Use of Your Home (Including Use by Daycare Providers)*. Can be downloaded via the Internet from: www.irs.ustreas.gov.

Note: In order to read and/or print the publication, you will need Acrobat Reader, a software program that is available for free from Adobe (www.adobe.com). Download the publication, open Acrobat Reader, and then open the downloaded file.

purposes. This is figured by dividing the area used for business by the total area of your home. For example, if your home measures 2,000 square feet and you are using 500 square feet for your home office, you will be able to deduct 25 percent of expenses such as rent, mortgage, interest, depreciation, taxes, insurance, utilities, and repairs. There are also other issues to be considered pertaining to the legalities of deductions. You will have to spend some time familiarizing yourself with them.

Increasing Your Chances for Success

If you are going to operate out of your home, there are several things you can do to ensure you will be more successful. Home offices have long been under scrutiny by many who wish to question their credibility. The following pages will discuss some of the issues that may make the difference between success and failure.

Organize Your Work Space

Setting aside your work space is not only an IRS requirement, but a necessary element of any business. It is important to understand that a home-based business is the same as a business in a commercial location with the exception of some special tax considerations. That's exactly the way you should treat it.

Organize your work space in an efficient manner and eliminate non-work items so you will not be tempted to mix the two during working hours. If you are operating a lawn mower repair shop out of your garage, don't use it to house your cars, bicycles, freezer, and old clothes. If you have an

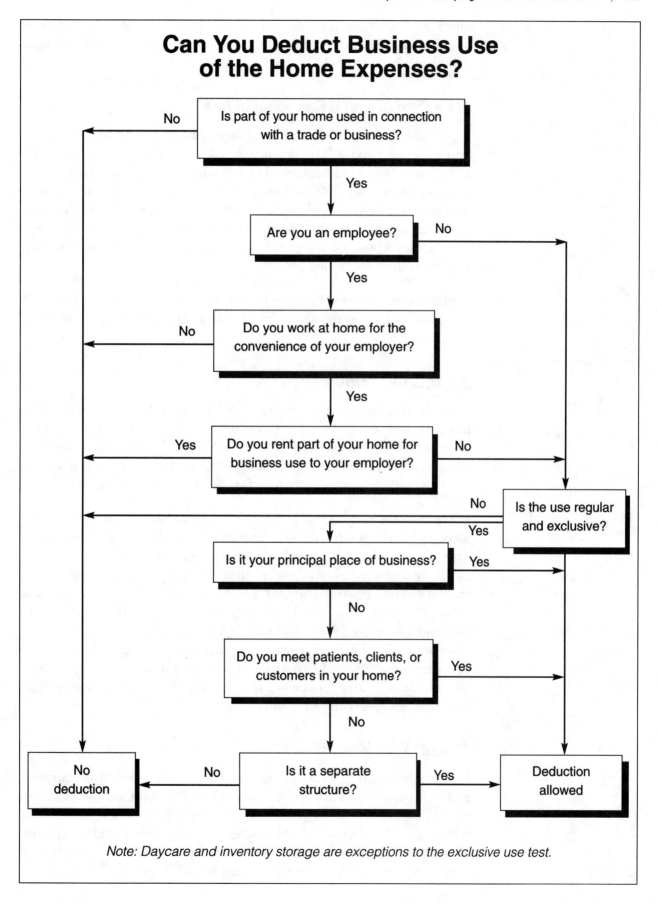

Can You Deduct Business Use of the Home Expenses?

Is part of your home used in connection with a trade or business?

No → (to No deduction)
Yes ↓

Are you an employee?

No → (to Is the use regular and exclusive?)
Yes ↓

Do you work at home for the convenience of your employer?

No → (to No deduction)
Yes ↓

Do you rent part of your home for business use to your employer?

Yes → (to No deduction)
No → (to Is the use regular and exclusive?)

Is the use regular and exclusive?

No → (to No deduction)
Yes ↓

Is it your principal place of business?

Yes → Deduction allowed
No ↓

Do you meet patients, clients, or customers in your home?

Yes → Deduction allowed
No ↓

Is it a separate structure?

No → No deduction
Yes → Deduction allowed

Note: Daycare and inventory storage are exceptions to the exclusive use test.

office in your family room, get rid of the TV, pool table, exercise machine, and ironing board. When a customer steps through the door into your office, it should feel like a business.

Take Care of Legal Responsibilities

A home business has the same legal requirements as any other business. You will still need a business license, DBA, seller's permit, etc. You should never mix your business finances with your personal finances. An effective recordkeeping system will have to be set up and you will need to find an accounting professional who can help you to maximize your tax benefits and prepare your final tax return. Set-up a separate bank account and a business telephone. You will need business insurance tailored to your products and services.

In other words, pretend that you have just opened business in a commercial location and do the same things you would have to do to get your business underway.

Set Business Hours

It will be very important for you to establish regular business hours. Credibility is hard to come by, but especially if you work out of your home. Your customers will take you more seriously if they see you are operating on a schedule. If you are not available when they call, you will soon find that they will be looking elsewhere for the same service or product.

When you are required to be away from your business during normal working hours, be sure you have provided a way to take messages and be sure to return your customers' calls. Invest in a good answering machine and leave a new message telling when you will be back in your office and assuring customers that you will return their calls. I knew one business owner who continually left the message, "I am away from my office right now and will return in two hours." The problem was that the caller never knew what time the message was left or when the two hours would be up. A better message would have been, "I have an appointment with a client and will be back in my office at 2 PM." Also be sure to ask for a name and phone number and offer to return the call.

Protect Your Work Hours

Inform your family and friends that you are serious about your business and will need to work without interruption. For some reason, a home-based business is usually perceived as being a place where visitors are welcome to show up and stay for a friendly visit. They would never think of popping into a corporate office for a cup of coffee, but surely you would welcome a break in your working hours! We wish we had a nickel for all the times when we have had to work late into the night because well-meaning friends decided we needed their company during the day.

Unfortunately, this is one of the most serious problems encountered in home-based businesses and one that is difficult to solve. It not only applies to family and friends, but to some of your customers who are anxious to establish a friendly relationship. We have used every trick in the book to get rid of unwanted visitors without offending them. We have resorted to proclaiming nonexistent appointments, calling each other from a telephone in the other room, walking the visitor slowly out the door, and any other means within our imaginations. When all else fails, tell the truth and it might just work.

Protect Your Free Hours

In addition to protecting your business hours, you will also have to decide what days and hours you wish to be closed and promise yourself you will use them for non-business pursuits. Guard that free time with your life.

Be sure to inform your customers of your working hours. If they want to come during your off hours, tell them nicely but firmly that you are closed. Most will respect you and return during your regular business hours.

At the end of your working day, turn on your answering machine and shut the door to your business. Plan activities with your family or friends and try not to overwhelm them with your business problems. The idea is to have fun and give yourself a break. You will soon feel overwhelmed and tired of your business if you never have the opportunity to get away from it.

It would be naive to pretend that a business owner will never have to work extra hours to make the business prosper. We probably ignore our own advice in this area more frequently than most. Do what you need to do to run your business, but don't let it run you. And don't let it cause you to burn out your enthusiasm and create problems with the people you care about. Remember, owning your own business is supposed to be a plus in your life!

Be Self-Disciplined

Owning your own business requires a great deal of time and effort. We have heard potential business owners exclaim they are going to quit working eight hours a day for a company and be free to set their own hours. It is true that you can decide on your hours. However, working for yourself will probably be equivalent to holding down two jobs, at least for the first three or four years until the business is functioning smoothly. For this reason, it will be necessary to develop a high degree of self-discipline.

Be willing to work long hours when it is necessary. If an extra effort is needed to get a job done, you will have to do it. Decide what hours you are willing to work and stick to your schedule. Don't fall into the trap of thinking you have free time. You are your own boss and you will have to treat yourself as you would an employee.

Dress for Success

Just because you are working at home, don't use it as an excuse to be a slob. Every trade has an acceptable mode of dress that should be adhered to. A home business is the perfect target for a 24-hour-a-day onslaught by customers. They will call on the telephone and ring the doorbell seven days a week from dawn to dark—and that includes holidays. No one can see what you look like on the other end of the phone, but if you are going to answer the door, look like a business person.

A client of ours tells a story of one day when she started working at 8 AM but was still in her bathrobe at 10 AM when a customer rang the doorbell. She hid behind the door and lost the customer. A customer can become turned off to businesses because the owners did not act and look like they could get the job done. If your customer is going to have confidence in your products or services, he or she must first have confidence in you. You are your best advertisement.

Be Totally Credible

Home-based business has come to represent a large segment of today's workforce and a powerful force in the economy. In fact, due in a large part to modern technology, almost every kind of business imaginable is being run out of a home office somewhere. Unfortunately, those same home businesses are often regarded as "little hobbies." Both of us were in home-based businesses long before we started teaching business classes and writing and publishing business books. It would probably be impossible to count the times we were told what wonderful hobbies we had. We liked our businesses, but can assure you that our reasons for being in business were measured in dollars as well as fun.

The truth is that a home-based business owner will have to expend extra effort to prove credibility and attract customers. Many professional business organizations, including chambers of commerce, are forming focus groups to help overcome this stigma. Meanwhile, professionalism is the only weapon that can be effectively used to overcome misconceptions about the seriousness of this major economic force.

Choosing a Legal Structure

One of the most important decisions you will make is how to legally structure your business. There are advantages and disadvantages to each form of organization. The type of legal format you choose will depend on the following factors:

- ✦ Your need for capital
- ✦ Your type of business
- ✦ When you want to start your business
- ✦ Your ability to finance your business
- ✦ The number of people involved in the business
- ✦ The liabilities and risks you are willing to assume
- ✦ Your personal tax situation
- ✦ Your plan for taking money out of the business
- ✦ Your plan for continuing the business if something should happen to you
- ✦ Your long-range business plan

✦ ✦ ✦ ✦

There are four different ways to organize your business: the sole proprietorship, the partnership, the corporation, and the limited liability company. The legal structure you choose will determine how much paper work you will have to do, how much personal liability you will incur, how you will be able to raise money, and how your business will be taxed.

Sole Proprietorship

This is the easiest, least expensive and least regulated business legal structure. A sole proprietorship is owned and operated by one person although it may have employees.

Advantages

- ◆ *Ease of formation.* There are fewer legal restrictions associated with forming a sole proprietorship.
- ◆ *Sole owner of the profits.* All profits go to you, the owner, as do the losses!
- ◆ *Least expensive to establish.* Costs vary according to the city in which the business is formed, but usually include a license fee and may include a business tax. This information can be obtained by calling the business license bureau of the city government. If you live in an unincorporated area, contact the county offices.
- ◆ *Fewer records are needed with a minimum of regulations.* While regulations vary by state, a sole proprietorship can generally be established by registering the company's name (filing a DBA) and by obtaining a business license.
- ◆ *Taxed as an individual.* As the sole owner, your business profit and loss is recorded on Federal Tax Form 1040, Schedule C, and the bottom line amount is transferred to your personal tax form. You will also file Schedule SE, which is your contribution to Social Security.
- ◆ *Total control.* The business is owned and operated by one person. All decision-making is vested in you as the owner. You have total responsibility and control.

Disadvantages

- ◆ *Unlimited personal liability.* You will be responsible for the full amount of business debt, which may exceed the investment. This liability extends to all assets such as your home and vehicle.
- ◆ *Less available capital.* Funding must come from the proprietor and obtaining long-term financing may be difficult. Loans are based on the strengths of the individual.
- ◆ *Limited growth potential.* The future of the company is dependent upon your capabilities in terms of knowledge, drive, and financial potential.
- ◆ *Heavy responsibility.* You are the only person responsible for the business. There will be no requisitions to central supply when you run out of envelopes. You will be responsible for evaluating office equipment and making the buying decisions. You have the ultimate

Loan: money lent with interest.

responsibility for the purchase of supplies, equipment, advertising, and insurance. You will also handle employees, marketing, bill paying, and customer relations.

◈ ***Death, illness, or injury can endanger the business.*** The business ceases to exist as a legal entity upon the death of the owner.

The sole proprietorship is best suited for a single owner business where taxes or product liability are not a concern. Because the entity is inseparable from the owner, the main disadvantages of this structure are unlimited liability, no tax benefits, and dissolution upon the death of the owner. The owner is responsible for taxes and files a Schedule C with Form 1040. The sole proprietorship is the most common form of business and comprises 70 percent of all American business entities. Many who are just starting a business choose this form until it becomes practical to enter into a partnership or to incorporate.

Partnership

A partnership is a legal business relationship in which two or more people agree to share ownership and management of a business. Often a partner is chosen for the skills or expertise you may lack. Sharing ownership of a business may be a way to gain more start-up money. Evaluate the advantages and disadvantages of this legal structure before making a decision.

Advantages

◈ ***Ease of formation.*** The legal requirements and expenses are fewer than those involved with forming a corporation. While regulations vary by state, a partnership can generally be established by registering the company's name (filing a DBA) and by obtaining a business license.

◈ ***Shared responsibility.*** Two or more heads are better than one! By sharing in the profits, partners are motivated to succeed. This form of legal structure allows for distribution of the work load and for sharing of ideas, skills, and responsibilities.

◈ ***Increased growth potential.*** A partnership makes it possible to obtain more capital and to tap into more skills.

◈ ***Ease of operation.*** The partnership has more freedom from government control and special taxation than the corporation.

Disadvantages

◈ ***Unlimited personal liability.*** Owners are personally responsible for the business debt. A partnership is not a separate legal entity, even though its income is reported on a separate informational tax return

Profit: financial gain, returns over expenditures.

(Form 1065). Profits must be included on each partner's individual tax return according to their percentage of interest in the business.

◈ *Lack of continuity.* Like the sole proprietorship, the partnership terminates upon the death or the withdrawal of a general partner unless the partnership agreement provides otherwise. Death, withdrawal, or bankruptcy of one partner endangers the entire business.

◈ *Relative difficulty in obtaining large sums of capital.* While the opportunity for getting long-term financing is greater in a partnership, it is still dependent on review of each individual partner's assets.

◈ *Difficulty in disposing of the partnership interest.* The buying out of a partnership or sale to another party must be spelled out in the partnership agreement.

◈ *Distribution of responsibility in bankruptcy.* In case of bankruptcy, the partner with more personal assets will lose more.

◈ *Partner's responsibility.* Each general partner can act on behalf of the company in conducting business. Each partner represents the company and can individually hire employees, borrow money, and operate the business. Choose someone you trust; you will be bound by each other's decisions.

◈ *Profits.* Profits are shared among the partners according to the terms set out in the partnership agreement.

A partnership is best suited for a business with two or more owners where taxes and product liability are not a concern. The entity is inseparable from the owners but can have property and debt in its name. There are no tax benefits and the partnership legally dissolves on change or death of a partner. Partners are responsible for filing taxes and use Form 1065.

There are different types of partnerships dependent on how active a role partners play in the business. **General partners** share equally in the responsibility for managing and financing the business. They also share equally in the liability. **Limited partners** risk only their investment in the business and are not subject to the same liabilities as a general partner as long as they do not participate in the management and control of the enterprise.

Debt: refers to borrowed funds and is generally secured by collateral or a co-signer; that which is owed.

This business structure is used as a way of raising capital to run the business. General partners can take on limited partners as a means of raising cash without involving outside investors in the management of the business. The general partners remain liable for the business' debt. A limited partnership is more expensive to create, involves extensive paper work, and is used mainly for companies that invest in real estate or speculative ventures.

Care should be taken when choosing a partner. This is a close working relationship and you must look carefully at the work style, character, personality, financial situation, skill, and expertise of your potential partner.

Partnership Agreements

Do not underestimate the need for a partnership agreement. Many friendships and good working relationships have ended over business disagreements. When financial considerations enter the picture, friendships are often put aside. Take some time and carefully prepare a partnership agreement and have it notarized. It will serve as the guideline for your working relationship with your partners. It will outline the financial, managerial, and material contributions by the partners into the business and delineate the roles of the partners in the business relationship.

The following are some subjects often covered in a partnership agreement:

- ◆ The purpose of the partnership business
- ◆ The terms of the partnership
- ◆ The goals of the partners and the partnership
- ◆ The financial contributions made by each partner for start-up and during the lifetime of the business
- ◆ The distribution of profits and losses
- ◆ The withdrawal of contributed assets or capital by a partner
- ◆ The management powers and work responsibilities of each partner
- ◆ The provisions for admitting new partners
- ◆ The provisions for expelling a partner
- ◆ The provisions for continuing the business in the event of a partner's death, illness, disability, or desire to leave
- ◆ The provision for determining the value of a departing partner's interest and method of payment of that interest
- ◆ The methods of settling disputes through mediation or arbitration
- ◆ The duration of the agreement and the terms of dissolution of the business

A Partnership Agreement is a contract that states how you want your business relationship to work. The Uniform Partnership Act (UPA) is a body of law that establishes the most basic legal rules applicable to partnerships. It has been adopted in all states except Louisiana. However, these rules can be changed by statements in your partnership agreement. Unless the agreement itself specifies a different date, a written agreement is effective when it is signed.

Corporation

The corporation is the most complex of the business structures. A corporation is a distinct legal entity, separate from the individuals who own it. It is formed by the authority of the state government, with approval from the Secretary of State. If business is conducted in more than one state, you must comply with the federal laws regarding interstate commerce. Federal and state laws may vary considerably.

Advantages

Stock: an ownership share in a corporation; another name for a share. Another definition would be accumulated merchandise.

- ◆ *Ownership is readily transferable.* The corporation does not cease to exist with the death of an owner.
- ◆ *Increased options for growth and fundraising.* A corporation has access to numerous investors and can raise substantial capital through the sale of stock.
- ◆ *The corporation is a separate legal entity.* It is responsible and liable for all debts. The shareholders are liable only for the amount they have invested. A corporation has an existence apart from the people who own it.
- ◆ *Authority can be delegated.* The corporation has the ability to draw on the expertise and skills of more than one individual.

Disadvantages

Net: what is left after deducting all expenses from the gross.

- ◆ *Extensive government regulations.* Corporations are complex to manage and are highly regulated. Burdensome local, state, and federal reports must be filed and regular stockholder meetings must be held.
- ◆ *Expensive to form and maintain.* The fees for setting up a corporate structure, the costs of stockholders' meetings, and the expense for legal fees and paperwork are some of the costs unique to the corporation.
- ◆ *Increased tax load.* Income tax is paid on the corporate net income (profit) and on individual salaries and dividends.

Because of the complexity of the corporation, you may wish to consult an attorney regarding its formation. Whether you choose to form the corporation on your own or with legal help, you will have to consider the following items in order to be knowledgeable and prepared.

Certificate of Incorporation

The preparation of a **certificate of incorporation** is generally the first step to incorporating. Many states have a standard certificate of incorporation form that may be used by small businesses. Copies may be obtained from the state official who grants charters or from larger stationers or office suppliers. The following information is usually required:

- ◈ *Corporate name of the company.* The name chosen must not be similar to any other corporation authorized to do business in the state. The name must not be deceptive so as to mislead the public. To be certain that the name you select is suitable, check the name availability through the designated state official in each state where you intend to do business before drawing up the certificate of incorporation.

- ◈ *Purposes of the corporation.* Purposes should be broad enough to allow for expansion and specific enough to give a clear idea of the business to be performed. Reference books and certificates of existing corporations are available at your local library and can provide examples of such clauses.

- ◈ *Length of time the corporation will exist.* The term may cover a number of years or be "perpetual."

- ◈ *Names and addresses of incorporators.* In some areas, at least one or more of the incorporators is required to be a resident of the state in which the corporation is being organized.

- ◈ *Location of the registered office of the corporation in the state of incorporation.* If you decide to obtain your charter from another state, you will be required to have an office there. You may appoint an agent in that state to act for you.

- ◈ *Proposed capital structure.* State the maximum amount and type of capital stock your corporation wishes authorization to issue. State the amount of capital required at the time of incorporation.

- ◈ *Management.* State the provisions for the regulation of the internal affairs of the corporation.

- ◈ *Director.* Provide the name and address of the person who will serve as the director until the first meeting of the stockholders.

Agent: a person who is authorized to act for or represent another person in dealing with a third party.

The charter will be issued when and if the designated state official determines that the name is available, that the certificate has been completely and properly executed, and that there has been no violation of state law.

In order to complete the incorporation process, the stockholders must meet. They must elect a board of directors and adopt by-laws. The board of directors will in turn elect the officers who will actually have charge of operating the corporation. Usually, the officers include a president, a secretary and a treasurer. In small corporations, the members of the board of directors are frequently elected as officers of the corporation.

Board of directors: those individuals elected by the stockholders of a corporation to manage the business.

Bylaws

The bylaws of the corporation may repeat some of the provisions of the charter and usually cover such items as the following:

- The location of the principal office and other offices
- The time, location, and notice of stockholder meetings
- Number of directors, their compensation, terms of office, method of election, and the filling of vacancies
- The time and location of directors' meetings
- Quorum and voting methods
- Insurance and form of stock certificates
- Methods of selecting officers and of designating their titles, duties, terms of office, and salaries
- Method of paying dividends
- Decisions regarding the fiscal year
- Procedure for amending the bylaws

In general, the cost and complexity of the corporate legal structure make it an unrealistic option for many small businesses.

S Corporation

There is a legal structure called the S Corporation status, which allows the small business corporation to have its income taxed to the shareholders as if the corporation were a partnership. One objective is to overcome the double tax feature of our system of taxing corporate income and stockholder dividends separately. There are specific conditions for making and maintaining an S Corporation election.

- The corporation must have 75 or fewer shareholders, all of whom are individuals or estates.
- There are no nonresident alien shareholders.
- There is only one class of outstanding stock.
- All shareholders consent to the election of S Corporation.
- A specific portion of the corporation's receipts must be derived from active business rather than passive investments.
- No limit is placed on the size of the corporation's income and assets.

Talk to your attorney or accountant to determine if this form of legal structure is right for your business.

Limited Liability Company (LLC)

The Limited Liability Company (LLC) is a relatively new form of business legal structure. It is a hybrid entity that allows owners the protection from personal liability provided to the corporate structure and the pass-through taxation of the partnership. The LLC does have some disadvantages. Because it is a new entity, laws regarding the LLC are still evolving and some issues regarding its operation remain unsettled. It is usually taxed as a partnership, but can be taxed as a corporation in some states. When taxed as a partnership, business owners can lose some company funded benefits.

Advantages

- ◆ *More liberal loss deductions.* The owners of an LLC do not assume liability for the business's debt and any losses can be used as tax deductions against active income. Loss deductions are more limited under an S Corporation than under an LLC.
- ◆ *More stock options.* LLCs can offer several different classes of stock with different rights.
- ◆ *Less restriction on participation.* There are no restrictions on the number or type of owners. An unlimited number of individuals, corporations, and/or partnerships may participate in an LLC.

Disadvantages

- ◆ *Difficulty in business expansion out of state.* If a company doing business in a state that allows LLCs decides to do business in another state without similar legislation, there is no provision for them to legally register to conduct business in the second state.
- ◆ *Transferability restriction test.* Ownership interests cannot be transferred to other parties without some restrictions.
- ◆ *Lack of uniform code.* In some states, the business is dissolved on the death, retirement, resignation, or expulsion of an owner. Some states impose a corporate tax on LLCs.
- ◆ *Restriction on type of business.* An LLC cannot be used for professional services such as an accountant, attorney, or insurance agent.

To set up an LLC, you follow a path similar to the formation of a corporation. You must submit an article of organization and the appropriate filing fees to the Secretary of State in the state where your business is organized. Because states differ in the information required, it is wise to consult your attorney or accountant if you think the Limited Liability Company form of legal structure is right for your business.

General Considerations

In choosing your particular legal structure, you will want to give careful consideration to all of the options available and base your decision on a personal evaluation of the following items:

- ◈ *The size of risk.* Look at the amount of the owner's liability for debts and taxes under each structure. How much liability are you willing to assume? How would you want your earnings to be taxed?
- ◈ *The continuity of the business.* If something should unexpectedly happen to you, what would happen to your business?
- ◈ *Your access to capital.* How much money will you need to develop and run your business? Where will you get this money?
- ◈ *Your management skills.* What is your business experience? What are the skills and abilities you bring to the company?
- ◈ *Your purpose for starting a business.* What is your ultimate goal? What are the possibilities for business growth?

Management: The art of conducting and supervising a business.

Keep in mind that your initial choice of a business form doesn't have to be permanent. You can start out as a sole proprietor. As your business develops, you may wish to take on partners. As the risks of personal liability increase, you may wish to form a corporation. If you change the structure of an existing business, you must notify the Internal Revenue Service and your state tax agency. A sole proprietorship or a partnership must change legal form through the business license bureau, while corporations register with the office of the Secretary of State. The Small Business Administration publishes material covering each type of legal structure. If you are unsure about which type of business structure is best for your business, you may wish to consult an attorney who is knowledgeable about the various types of business organization.

TECH TIP 10

Internet Access to IRS Information on Starting a Business

The Internal Revenue Service provides specific business tax information for each form of legal structure. The IRS Web site homepage is located at:

www.irs.ustreas.gov/

Open this site and click on "Small Business Corner." You will be taken to another page with topics entitled "Before You Start Your Business," "Operating Your Business," "Small Business News," and "Employment Taxes." Subsequent pages can provide information on tax considerations for small business, recordkeeping considerations, and access to downloadable tax forms.

Presenting Your Business

A company's image is based primarily on its paper correspondence. Such identity materials as stationery, business cards, and envelopes convey a company's image.

From the first day you begin business, it will be necessary for you to have certain materials that represent your business, not only to your customers, but to suppliers and other business owners. When you are organizing your venture, you will be approaching suppliers, dealers, and other people in related businesses. It is important they perceive your business as having a base of stability. Otherwise, they may choose to ignore your requests. It is almost impossible to do the background work that needs to be done to develop a business without having cards and letterhead. You may also need a brochure of some type to begin advertising your business. The marketing and advertising of a business is covered in more detail in Chapter 19. In this chapter we will discuss developing your graphic identity through your printed materials.

◆ ◆ ◆ ◆

Graphic Identity

First impressions are lasting and often the first impression made by a business is through what is called "graphic identity." Graphic identity refers to the visual representation of your company. It includes the design of your logo and the style of your promotional materials.

A company's graphic or visual identity usually includes a logo, logotype (type style), and company colors. The combinations you choose will create your identity and will

TECH TIP 11
Use Technology to Test Your Logo

Technology provides you with many marketing opportunities; it is important that you view the appearance and acceptability of your logo, logotype, and color choices in these different formats. If your marketing materials are multi-colored, will they be expensive to reproduce? Will the design lose its impact when faxed and received as a black and white transmission? Photocopy your materials and see how the design holds up. Will the design reproduce well in different sizes? Will the logo on your brochure be just as effective on your letterhead and business card? If your logo is produced by an out-of-house graphic designer, be sure to get the logo in an electronic format that can be pasted into documents and put on the Web. View the design on the Web. How does it look on the screen? If it is very detailed and colorful, it may increase download time for your potential customers. Try to anticipate all future uses of your marketing materials and determine how they will stand up to electronic and telecommunication mediums.

make your promotional and packaging materials recognizable. In today's highly competitive world, it is important to be recognized, to be remembered and to be viewed as an established business.

A **logo** is a symbol that represents the company. It may be a monogram of the company's initials or a design. A logo is a quick way of getting people to notice and remember your business. When designing your logo, you want to be sure that it is appropriate to your business and that the art work is timely. You can design your own, select from standard logos available from a printer, hire a professional artist, or work with a high school or college art student. Be sure to consider registering your logo with the Copyright Office or the Patent and Trademark Office in Washington, DC. Refer to Chapter 9 regarding these protections. The addresses of these agencies are listed in Resources, page 209.

Logotype refers to the type style used in the writing of your business name. The type size, placement, and style can communicate a great deal about your company. There are hundreds of type styles and sizes available and, within each type family, there are plain, italic, and bold versions.

Often a company will wish to adopt **company colors**. Most often two colors are used. Just as with type style, the colors you choose can set the tone for your marketing materials. Make sure the colors fit your company and the "feel" you wish to project.

You may be a small company competing with larger companies or a new company entering an existing market. You need to look competent and established. A carefully planned and implemented graphic identity can give you the edge you need and should last for many years.

Business Cards

Business cards are one of the most universally used marketing tools. Not only do they give your business credibility, they serve as a visual reminder of you and your business. Be sure to have business cards printed as soon as possible. Whenever you attempt to deal with another business or individual, you should give them your card. This not only gives your business credibility, but the recipient now has a reminder of you and your business.

Begin to gather cards as you network in the business community, deal with suppliers, and evaluate competitors. When you have collected 30 to 40 of them, arrange them on a tabletop. Now scan the cards and see which ones catch your eye. Then evaluate the cards that caught your attention in terms of the following questions:

- What is it about this card that first draws your attention?
- Is the logo appropriate and descriptive?
- Is the company name legible?
- Is the contact person's name and phone number included?
- Does the card tell what product is offered?
- Does it tell the service provided?
- Does the card tell the location of the business?
- Is the overall appearance pleasing?
- Is the card one you will remember?

Ask these same questions of your card as you plan it. And keep in mind the following items:

- The logo must be appropriate and descriptive.
- The company name must be legible and in the correct type size.
- A contact person's name and phone number must appear on it.
- Include a statement about the product or service offered.
- The overall appearance of the card must be pleasing.
- The card should be one the customer will remember.

A business card is like a mini-billboard. It should tell the what, why, who, how, when, and where of your business.

Do not buy your first cards in large quantity. Even though the purchase of a large quantity of business cards will save you money on a per unit basis, 1,000 cards will do you no good if the information on your cards is no longer valid. They will just have to be discarded and the money you saved will be lost. In a very short time you may want to change your card for any number of reasons: change of address, addition of a logo, inclusion of a fax number, adding an e-mail address, or addition of new products or services. The evolution of the business cards for the company, Out of Your Mind...and Into the Marketplace™, is demonstrated on the **Business Card Development** example on page 78. As the location and nature of the business changed, the business card changed. All businesses change as they grow. By purchasing your cards in reasonable amounts, you can avoid having to discard ones that no longer apply to your situation.

Promotional Materials

A business card, the letterhead, and a brochure are the primary promotional materials of all businesses. Following is a listing of printed materials your company can use for business promotion and graphic identity presentation:

Brochures	Invoices
Building sign	Letterhead
Business cards	Mailing labels
Business reply envelopes	Name badges
Checks	Presentation folders
Contracts/agreements	Promotional give-aways
Display signs	Purchase orders
Envelopes	Uniforms
Flyers	Vehicle signs

We have already discussed the business card. The other printed material you will need is a **letterhead**. Your letterhead is your business stationery. It should be used for all business correspondence. It also lends credibility to your business. The color, type, and quality of the paper you use will reflect on your company. Expand the information formatted for your business card and develop a "look" that appears on all your promotional materials and carries over to your package design. Duplicate the format, type style, and colors used on your business card for continuity. When you have your letterhead printed, purchase a smaller quantity of second sheets. When writing a business letter, the letterhead is used only for the first page.

Brochures are essential for any business where the prospective customer needs detailed information about the qualifications and expertise of the owner and the services and products offered. More information can be supplied in a brochure than would be practical for a classified ad. Brochures can be mailed, distributed door to door, or given out at community events and trade shows. **Guidelines for Developing a Brochure** instruction sheet has been included on page 79 to help you develop your own brochure.

The above-mentioned are the main presentation materials used for a small business. As your business grows, you may want to develop other materials. If you are a retailer, have a catalog printed and mailed to your customers. You may even want to go into color processing. Signs may be needed for a display, your building, or a vehicle. To create a "total look" for your business, you can expand your graphic identity to include your business checks, mailing labels, purchase order forms, and invoices. For the small business just getting started, business cards, letterhead, a basic brochure, and an order form are enough to begin with. **Guidelines for Developing an Order Form** is included on page 80.

Choosing a Printer

Two of the major considerations in choosing a printer are quality of work and price. Sometimes the lowest bid is not the most cost effective. If the workmanship on the project and the quality of materials are poor, your business image will suffer. After all, the presentation materials you use often determine how your customers, suppliers, and competitors will perceive your business.

Quality and price vary among printers. You will want to visit three or four printers in your area. Get a price list and view samples of their work. You may have your cards and letterhead done at one shop and your brochures printed at another shop that specializes in that type of printed matter.

In order to save money, much of your printing can be done from camera-ready copy. This means that you take the printer a finished product ready to be reproduced. Note that camera-ready copy should only be used if you can make your layout look professional and businesslike. Desktop publishing companies can help you with this work.

Desktop publishing: commonly used term for computer-generated printed materials such as newsletters and brochures.

Before having your printing done, be sure to get an estimate in writing. A colleague was given a verbal quotation for printing booklets and boxes for a novelty item. Upon delivery, she paid the bill in full. A month later, she was surprised to receive another bill for setup charges. The printer's claim was that the setup charges covered setting up and inking the printing press and were separate. The business owner consulted an attorney and the outcome was that she was legally responsible for the additional charges. Since there was no written agreement, she was unable to prove her claim.

Business Card Development

The following examples illustrate how business cards were changed to add a logo and a fax number, to change addresses and phone numbers, and to reflect changes in the nature of a business. Out of Your Mind . . . And Into the Marketplace™ started as a small, home-based consulting service located in Fullerton, California. It later added a logo, expanded its service to include seminars and textbooks, and relocated the main office to Tustin, while opening another office in Camarillo, California. The business developed educational programs and business planning software and now offers business plan and publishing consulting. In order to grow, businesses must be dynamic. In order to keep your market informed, these changes must be reflected on that "mini-billboard" called the business card. Use judgment in quantity purchase of promotional materials.

OUT OF YOUR MIND . . . .
AND INTO THE MARKETPLACE
SMALL & HOME-BASED BUSINESS CONSULTING

JERRY JINNETT
&
LINDA PINSON

3031 Colt Way #223
Fullerton, CA 92633
Tel. No. (714) 523-1849

Small Business Consulting
Textbooks
Seminars

OUT OF YOUR MIND...
AND INTO THE MARKETPLACE™

LINDA PINSON
13381 WHITE SAND DRIVE
TUSTIN, CA 92680
Tel. No. (714) 544-0248

JERRY JINNETT
1734 SHORELINE STREET
CAMARILLO, CA 93010
Tel. No. (805) 484-2135

OUT OF YOUR MIND...
AND INTO THE MARKETPLACE™

PUBLISHER OF BUSINESS BOOKS & BUSINESS PLAN SOFTWARE

International Business Consulting
Business Plan Consulting
Business Education Programs

LINDA PINSON
President

13381 White Sand Drive
Tustin, CA 92680
Tel: (714) 544-0248
FAX: (714) 730-1414
EMail: LPinson@AOL.com

OUT OF YOUR MIND...
AND INTO THE MARKETPLACE™

AUTHORS OF BUSINESS BOOKS & BUSINESS PLAN SOFTWARE

Business Education Programs
Business Plan Consulting
Publishing Consulting

JERRY JINNETT
2824 Bedford Street
Johnstown, PA 15904

(814) 266-9187
CA Office: (714) 544-0248

Guidelines for Developing a Brochure

A brochure is a general term for a promotional piece that contains the following information about your business:

1. Company name: _____

   _____

2. Company address: _Be sure to include the full address and zip code._

   _____

   _____

   _____

3. Telephone, fax, and e-mail: _Be sure to include the area code. Also include your Web site if_ _you have one_

   _____

4. Key people: _Clients and customers want to know the background and expertise of the people with whom they will be doing business and feel more comfortable if they can ask for a contact person by name. You may wish to include short biographies of key people within your business. You may want to include photos._

5. Features: _Features are characteristics or attributes of your product or service. Features "tell" about your business._

   _____

   _____

6. Benefits: _Benefits "sell" your business. They describe the advantages of purchasing and using your product or service._

   _____

   _____

7. Statement of purpose: _Including the mission statement of your business can convey your business philosophy and goals to the customer._

   _____

8. Testimonials from satisfied customers: _____

   _____

   _____

   _____

Guidelines for Developing an Order Form

Most product and some service businesses will need an order form that tells a customer the terms of a sale. The following should serve as a guideline.

1. Business name: _____

2. Business address: Be sure to include the full address and zip code. _____
   _____

   _____

3. Telephone, fax, and e-mail: Be sure to include the area code. Also include your Web site ___
   if you have one. _____

4. Name of contact person: Customers prefer to ask for an individual when they call. ___
   _____

5. Photos or drawings of your product or a representation of your service: _____
   _____

6. Description of your product or service: _____
   _____

7. Price list: Indicate whether price is wholesale or retail. Indicate any quantity discounts. ___
   _____

8. Terms of payment: _____
   a. Net 30: Invoice must be paid in full within 30 days. _____
   b. Net 30, 2%/10: Invoice to be paid in full in 30 days. If paid within 10 days, a 2% ___
       discount can be taken on the bill excluding the shipping charges. _____
   c. COD (Cash on delivery): Invoice is to be paid to the delivery agent on receipt of goods. ___
   d. Proforma: Goods will be shipped after receipt of full payment. _____

9. Return policy: You may wish to include a statement as follows: "Returns and/or adjustments ___
   must be made within 14 days of receipt of goods." Use a time frame of your choice. ___

10. Shipping terms: FOB origin would mean that the customer pays shipping charges and ___
    assumes the responsibility for the goods from the time they leave your business. ___
    Example: FOB Tustin, CA. _____

11. Minimum order policy: Can be a dollar or unit amount. _____
    _____

12. Warranty and/or guarantee: _____
    _____

Protecting Your Business

W̲e all have great ideas for new products or services and usually keep these ideas stashed away in the back of our minds. We think they are silly or we are afraid that if we do disclose them, the idea will be stolen. Don't worry about "silly." Remember the Pet Rock! Don't let the fear of having your idea stolen keep you from the marketplace. In order to develop and sell ideas, you have to disclose them.

❖ ❖ ❖ ❖ ❖

When you are developing your business, you want to make certain that you are not infringing on the rights of others. You also want to get protection for your own work.

Disclosure Letter

One way of protecting your idea is through the use of a disclosure letter. This is a letter outlining your idea for your new product or service, detailing the research and work you have done to date and citing the people you have contacted while doing your research. Date the letter and have it notarized. The purpose of the disclosure letter is to verify the date on which the idea was yours. Place the letter in a sealed envelope and file it in a safe place.

Journal

Establishing a date by means of a disclosure letter is not enough. You must be able to demonstrate that you are involved in an active business as opposed to a passive business activity. An active business is able to show continuous work and progress in developing the idea into a viable product or service. This may be done by keeping a **log or journal**. This is a diary in which you verify ongoing work through daily entries. To be considered a legal document, the journal must be a bound book (not loose-leaf), have consecutively numbered pages, be written in ink, and contain no erasures. If you make an error, line through it, initial it and make the correction. Do not use correction fluid. Include information regarding the people to whom you have spoken about your idea and the dates and locations of the meetings. The journal and the disclosure letter give you the security you need to begin your market research. You may be able to get further protection through a copyright, trademark, or patent. A **Sample Journal Page** with entries has been included at the end of this chapter.

Copyright

A **copyright** is a legal protection provided to the authors of "original works of authorship that are fixed in a tangible form of expression." The fixation does not need to be directly perceptible, so long as it may be communicated with the aid of a machine or device. Copyrightable works include the following categories:

- ◈ Literary works
- ◈ Musical works, including any accompanying words
- ◈ Dramatic works, including any accompanying music
- ◈ Pantomimes and choreographic works
- ◈ Pictorial, graphic, and sculptural works
- ◈ Motion pictures and other audiovisual works
- ◈ Sound recordings
- ◈ Architectural works
- ◈ Electronic media

These categories cover a broad area. You may have difficulty determining the category to register your work in. A phone call to the Copyright Office can clarify this for you. An address and phone number for the Copyright Office has been included in Resources, p. 209.

Under the present law, copyright protection is secured automatically when the work is created, and a work is "created" when it is fixed in a copy or phonorecord for the first time. "Copies" are material objects from which a work can be read or visually perceived either directly or with the aid of a machine or device such as books, manuscripts, sheet music, film, videotape, or microfilm. "Phonorecords" are material objects that embody fixations of sounds such as audio tapes and phonograph disks.

For works first published on and after March 1, 1989, the use of the copyright notice is optional although highly recommended. Before March 1, 1989, the use of the notice was required on all published works and any work first published before that date must bear a notice or risk loss of copyright protection.

Use of the notice is recommended because it informs the public that the work is protected by copyright, identifies the copyright owner and shows the year of the first publication. The notice for visually perceptible copies should contain all of the following three elements:

1. *The symbol* © (the letter c in a circle), or the word "Copyright," or the abbreviation "Copr."
2. *The year of first publication* of the work.
3. *The name of the owner of copyright* in the work or an abbreviation by which the name can be recognized, or a generally known alternative designation of the owner.

Example: ©2000 Jane Doe

The "c in a circle" notice is used only on "visually perceptible copies." Certain types of works such as musical, dramatic, and literary works may be fixed by means of sound in an audio recording.

Generally, no publication or registration in the Copyright Office is required to secure a copyright. There are, however, certain advantages to registration.

◆ Registration establishes a public record of the copyright claim.

◆ Before an infringement suit may be filed in court, registration is necessary for works of U.S. origin and for foreign works not originating in a Berne Union Country. (For clarification, request Circular 93 from the Copyright Office.)

◆ If made before or within five years of publication, registration will establish prima facie evidence in court of the validity of the copyright and of the facts stated in the certificate.

◆ If registration is made within three months after publication of the work or prior to an infringement of the work, statutory damages and attorney's fees will be available to the copyright owner in court actions.

◆ Copyright registration allows the owner of the copyright to record the registration with the U.S. Customs Service for protection against the importation of infringing copies.

Registration may be made at any time within the life of the copyright.

TECH TIP 12
Copyright, Patent, and Trademark Information via the Internet

The Library of Congress Web site at lcweb.loc.gov/copyright/circs/ provides access to copyright information circulars, factsheets, and form letters. Browse through the information listings and view text to determine protection that may be available for your printed or graphic work. Through links from the home page, regulation requirements and registration forms can be printed. Information is available in Adobe Acrobat PDF format, which can be downloaded free from the site.

The U.S. Patent and Trademark Office Web site is located at www.uspto.gov/. The site's homepage provides links to specific information on the trademark and patent processes. For example, clicking on "Patents" takes you to a page that allows you to search U.S. patent databases. Clicking on "Trademarks" takes you to a page that allows you to apply online or to check on the status of a trademark application. A menu on the homepage provides links to databases, search criteria, information on fee structures, and downloadable instructions and registration forms.

To register a work, send the following three elements in the same envelope or package to the Copyright Office. The address is listed in the Resources section at the end of this book.

- ◈ A properly completed application form. (Free application forms are supplied by the Copyright Office.)
- ◈ A nonrefundable filing fee of $30 effective through June 30, 2002. Copyright fees are adjusted at intervals, based on increases in the Consumer Price Index. Contact the Copyright Office for the current fee schedule.
- ◈ A nonreturnable deposit of the work being registered. The deposit requirements vary in particular situations and special deposit requirements exist for many types of works. If you are unsure of the deposit requirement for your work, write or call the Copyright Office and describe the work you wish to register.

A copyright registration is effective on the date the Copyright Office receives all of the required elements in the acceptable form, regardless of how long it then takes to process the application and to mail the certificate of registration. The copyright protection is for the life of the author plus an additional 50 years after the author's death. The use of the copyright notice is the responsibility of the copyright owner and does not require advance permission or registration with the Copyright Office.

Trademark

A **trademark** is a word, symbol, unique name, design, logo, slogan or some combination of these used by a company to identify its products. A **service mark** identifies and distinguishes a service rather than a product. A **trade name** is used to designate a company rather than a product or service. In general, the federal trademark statute covers trademarks, service marks, and words, names, or symbols that identify or are capable of distinguishing goods or services. Copyright registration cannot be made for names, titles, and other short phrases or expressions.

Until recently, trademark and service mark rights were granted based on use. An application to register a trademark in the U.S. could only be made if the mark had actually been used for a product or service that had been offered for sale through interstate commerce. Recent changes in the U.S. trademark law now allow a company or individual to file a trademark application for the purpose of "reserving" that trademark for future licensing and to protect the trademark for up to three years before it is actually used in commerce. These are known as "intent-to-use" applications.

Trademark renewals take place every ten years. There is a fee for renewal and a penalty for late renewal applications.

Although there is no requirement to file, registration provides certain legal protection to trademark owners in the United States. Application and filing forms are available from the Patent and Trademark Office, which is listed in the Resources section. Registration requires three steps:

1. A properly completed registration form.
2. An application for registration fee. **Note:** The current minimum fee is $245. During the year 2000, the Patent and Trademark office will be considering legislative changes to adjust several patent and trademark fees. Patent and trademark customers may wish to refer to the official PTO Web site (www.uspto.gov) for the most current fee amounts.
3. A physical representation of the mark.

There is a standard format for the use of the trademark symbol. The letters "TM" (^{TM}) must be placed after every use of the trademark or symbol. The letters "SM" (^{SM}) are used for a service mark. Once the trademark registration has been completed and confirmed, the symbol R (®) with a circle around it will be placed after every use of the trademarked word or symbol.

These marks serve to identify and distinguish an owner's products, goods, or services from those of the competition. They can serve as good marketing tools provided the quality and reputation of goods and services are maintained.

Patent

When you have an idea for a new invention or process, it is important to analyze that idea for originality and patentability. One of the most difficult and crucial steps to securing a patent is to determine "novelty." Establishing novelty involves two things:

1. Analysis according to specific standards set down by the Patent Office.
2. Determining if anyone has patented it first.

The only sure way to do this is to conduct a search of Patent Office files. To help make these files available to the public, the federal government established the Depository Library Program. These libraries offer the publications of the U.S. Patent Classification System, contain current issues of U.S. patents, maintain collections of earlier issued patents, and provide technical staff assistance in their use. A listing of Depository Libraries is available through the Government Printing Office. A search of patents can be informative. Besides indicating if your device is patentable, it may disclose patents better than yours, but not in production. You may be able to contact the inventor and arrange to have it manufactured and sold by your company.

Another service provided for inventors by the Patent Office is the acceptance and preservation for the papers disclosing an invention. This "disclosure document" is accepted as evidence of the dates of conception of the invention. It will be retained for two years. A fee must accompany the disclosure. It must also be accompanied by a self-addressed, stamped envelope and a duplicate copy signed by the inventor. The papers will be stamped with an identifying number and returned with the reminder that the disclosure document may be relied upon only as evidence of the date of conception and that an application must be filed in order to provide patent protection. During that time you must show continuous work and demonstrate that you are involved in an "active" as opposed to a "passive" process. This can be accomplished through the use of the journal, which was discussed earlier in this chapter.

An application for a patent is made to the Commissioner of Patents and Trademarks and includes the following:

◆ A written document, which comprises a specification (description and claims), and an oath or declaration
◆ A drawing when necessary
◆ A filing fee according to the fee schedule

Utility patent: may be granted to anyone who invents or discovers new, useful, and non-obvious process, machine, article of manufacture, or composition of matter.

Design patent: may be granted to anyone who invents a new, original, and ornamental design for an article of manufacture.

Plant patent: may be granted to anyone who invents or discovers and asexually reproduces any distinct and new variety of a plant.

The term of a patent is 17 years. A maintenance fee is due every $3\frac{1}{2}$, $7\frac{1}{2}$, and $11\frac{1}{2}$ years after the original grant for all patents issuing from the applications filed on and after December 12, 1980. The maintenance fee must be paid at the stipulated times to maintain the patent. After the patent has expired anyone may make, use, or sell the invention without permission of the patentee, provided that matter covered by other unexpired patents is not used.

The preparation of an application for a patent and the conducting of the proceedings in the Patent and Trademark Office to obtain that patent are undertakings that require a thorough knowledge of the scientific or technical matters involved in the particular invention as well as knowledge of the legal aspects of the patent process. Although inventors may prepare and file their own applications and may conduct their own proceedings, they may get into considerable difficulty. The patent process can be tedious, complicated, and lengthy. Most inventors employ the services of registered patent attorneys or patent agents. However, it is to your advantage to be as knowledgeable as possible about the patenting process. The address for the Patent Office is included in the Resources section in the back of the book.

Provisional Patent Application

Since June of 1995, the U.S. Patent and Trademark Office (PTO) has offered inventors the option of filing a provisional application for patent. The process was designed to provide a lower cost for first patent filing in the U.S. and to give U.S. applicants parity with foreign applicants under the GATT Uruguay Round Agreements. This also allows individual inventors to show their inventions to potential manufacturers and investors without fear of having their ideas stolen. To be complete, a provisional application must include a cover sheet, a written description of the invention, any drawings necessary to understand the invention, and the names of all inventors. The usual fee is $150 but a reduced fee of $75 is available for inventors who have established small entity status as independent inventors or small businesses with the PTO.

This process does not replace the need for applying for a regular patent. The applicant must file a non-provisional application to obtain a patent prior to the PPA expiration date. The PPA is good for one year.

Contracts

Another way to protect your business interests is through a contract. Businesses enter into various types of agreements and contracts with employees, vendors, customers, and partners. A contract is an agreement between two or more people, which creates an obligation to do or not to do something in exchange for money or some other consideration. Although an oral contract may be enforceable if its material terms can be proven, confusion can be avoided by creating a written document that provides evidence of the parties' agreements or non-agreements.

From a legal standpoint, many of the papers generated by a business are considered contracts. For example, a purchase order is a contract. In some cases, letters are considered contracts whose wording can be legally binding on a company. One of the most common forms of contract entered into by a new business is a lease. A lease is a contract between the owner of the building (lessor or landlord) and the occupant of the building (lessee or tenant). A lease sets forth the terms and conditions under which the tenant may occupy the building or space and the obligations of each of the parties. The subject of lease provisions has been covered in Chapter 5. Following are some other common situations requiring contracts:

◈ Bank or individual loans
◈ Sale or purchase of equity
◈ Sale or purchase of a business
◈ Sale or purchase of real estate
◈ Sale or purchase of product or service
◈ Insurance policies
◈ Long-term buying arrangement
◈ Long-term selling arrangement
◈ Partnership agreement
◈ Lease of property, or equipment
◈ Employee contracts

Develop a habit of keeping written records of important meetings and phone conversations. If anything is said in a conversation with a vendor, customer, or business contact, send a confirming letter documenting what has been said. If the need arises, you will have a permanent record you can refer to later.

Hiring an Attorney

Hiring an attorney is an expense that many business owners would like to avoid. However, saving on legal costs now may cost you more in the long run if a dispute, disagreement, or violation of a legal requirement occurs in the future. You will probably want to retain an attorney to prepare your partnership agreement or to set up your corporation or LLC.

You may also want to consult with an attorney to be sure you are obtaining the necessary licenses and permits for your type of business.

In most cases, the best way to find an attorney is through a referral from a banker, an accountant, or business associate. The local bar association or legal referral service can also put you in touch with attorneys in your area.

Be sure the attorney you retain is qualified in the area of work you need done. Look for someone who is familiar with small business. If you need specialized assistance such as tax, labor, or patent law, ask an attorney for a referral to a specialist. Many trade and professional associations provide lists of attorneys that specialize in their areas of concern.

Once you find an attorney, get everything in writing. Fees and arrangements, the nature of the legal services to be provided, and attorney/client responsibilities must be understood to avoid misunderstandings.

Remember that the decisions you make about your business will be your own. An attorney can inform you regarding your options and the legal ramifications of those choices.

Sample Journal Page

Page 18

October 8, 2000: Adams Community College, Blair, NY: Took class in Basic Recordkeeping. Met with instructor, Linda Pinson, regarding consulting and setting up of my recordkeeping system.

October 11, 2000: Contacted Dan Jenkins at Adams Community College regarding teaching basic fly-fishing skills. We will jointly develop a questionnaire to be distributed to students in order to determine interest. (555) 555-7642.

October 18, 2000: Arranged to speak to the chamber of commerce on the subject "Alternative Sports" on Thursday, December 12, 2000 at The Market Restaurant. Contact: Jane Morgan (714) 555-9734. Will distribute questionnaire to determine interest in sporting goods store in this community.

October 26, 2000: Taught class, "Basic Fly-Fishing," from 7 to 9 PM at Adams Community College, Blair. Twenty-seven students attended, ages ranged from 18 to 52, interest from five students regarding a fishing trip: Sam Johnson 463-9728; Glenn Smith 743-9652; Sarah Bennett 462-8931; Suzanne Kim 426-9276; and David Kelley 626-6201.

November 1, 2000: Exhibited at Community Days in the park on Beach Street. Approximately 10,000 attended event. Conducted questionnaire interviews with 462 people responding as follows:

1. Previous fishing experience = 36
   Where: river = 12   ocean = 24
   Did you enjoy:
   Yes = 16 (supervised, safety equipment, skilled leader)
   No = 20 (poorly planned, off schedule, canceled with no refund)

2. Interest in fly-fishing classes = 216
   Evenings = 113
   Weekday = 26
   Saturday = 186

3. Interest in fishing trips = 36

4. What would you expect to pay:
   Range $35 to $50 for four hour class; $175 to $250 for two-day trip

5. Majority read Register (397), listen to KZLM radio (201), respond to coupons in Penny Saver (122).

November 8, 2000: Meeting scheduled for December 11 at 10:00 with Mr. Jim Anderson of SCORE to discuss developing a business plan.

Securing a Business License

CHAPTER 10

The first question you may ask is: why get a business license? If your business is going to operate within the law, it will be necessary for you to obtain a license or permit in the city or county you will be doing business in.

❖ ❖ ❖ ❖

If that business is service-related and performs any portion of its work in other cities outside of its operational center, you may also be required to buy licenses in those cities. For example, if you have a repair service and you make several calls to homes away from the city where your shop is located, you could be obligated to purchase business licenses in the cities you service. For occasional work in another city, you may only be required to obtain a permit for those days you perform the work.

Business licenses are serious matters in most cities. They provide a source of revenue for the city or county. Licensing is also a means of controlling the types of businesses that operate within their jurisdictions.

It is true that many businesses are currently operating without licenses. An early 1996 crackdown in one major city showed that almost 50 percent of its businesses failed to produce current business licenses. Fines were imposed and ultimatums issued that failure to secure licenses would result in shutdowns. A business license is inexpensive and lends credibility to your operation. Without one, you, too, run the risk of being discovered and fined and/or barred from doing any business at all.

Location Considerations

In Chapter 5, "Choosing a Business Location" you learned the basics of selecting the site of your business. Selecting your location and getting your business license is an interactive process. A business license is granted for a specific location and the selection of the location must take into account licensing restrictions.

Contact the City or County Clerk's office in the city or county where you wish to locate your base of operation. They are an excellent source of information regarding police, fire, and health permits needed for your business. Since any business location must fall within the zoning regulations, you may obtain verification from the zoning commission to determine if your business is approved for the location you have chosen. The local business license bureau can also help you with your decision by giving you information on any special restrictions as to types of businesses allowed or disallowed at any location.

If you have decided to locate in a shopping center or industrial area or other commercial location, call the chamber of commerce or city and ask for any publications with listings of facilities available showing number of square feet, price per square foot, and other pertinent information.

You may also contact the management of the commercial or industrial complex you are considering and request written information about that location and current availability of leasing space. You should be able to get detailed information as to lease terms, restrictions, traffic patterns and other demographics. Be sure to read carefully and understand all the terms contained in a lease agreement. They vary and may well spell the difference between profit and loss for your business.

Licensing a Home-Based Business

If you have elected to have a home-based business, restrictions may not permit you to get a business license to operate in your city. You may be forced to move your business outside the home or operate outside of the law. If your family happens to be moving and you are a seasoned entrepreneur, you may wish to select your home partly on the basis of whether or not that city's ordinances will allow you to operate your business—or any business—out of your home.

If you are planning on living in a planned community, don't forget to check into any restrictions the association may have that relate to business use of your home. Even if the city will allow you to operate your business, the association may preclude that option.

Different types of businesses may be subject to special restrictions by the city or county. For instance, a mail-order business may be allowed in your home, but a direct-sales operation may be prohibited. Repair services may be allowed, but only if they do not involve the use of toxic chemicals. Food services will probably be disallowed, but the city may allow you to use your home as an administrative office for your business.

In most cities and planned communities, home-based businesses are not permitted to change the appearance of the neighborhood and, therefore, you may be prohibited from the use of advertising or equipment that can be viewed from the street. Very often, police or fire inspections will be conducted to see that your business does not violate any of several restrictions.

Doing some diligent ground work ahead of time may eliminate the possibility of selecting a business location only to find later it was not an appropriate and/or legal choice.

> **Direct selling:** the process whereby the producer sells to the user, ultimate consumer, or retailer without intervening middlemen.

Applying for a Business License

Once you have determined that your business meets all the specific requirements for operation within the city or county you have chosen, you are ready for a trip to the Business License Bureau or the City or County Clerk's office to legalize your business.

You will be asked to fill out an application. Call ahead to find out what information you will need to complete the application. This will save you time and ensure that you have all of your information on hand when it is needed.

The application is usually fairly simple and will require only general information. You will probably be asked to supply such specifics as business name, names of owners, address of business, type of business, number of employees, expected gross income, vehicles to be operated, and any other relevant information.

A typical fee for a business may be as little as ten cents per $1,000 of projected revenues. We have also seen specific license fees applied to certain kinds of businesses. For instance, in one eastern city the charge for a home business license is $350.

You will probably be asked to leave your completed application together with one year's fee (frequently based on projected gross revenues).Your application will be reviewed by the proper agents and a license will either be issued or refused within a few days.

Business licenses are renewed annually, subject to that city or county's codes and regulations. Your renewal notice will be sent to you, but it is your responsibility to renew should you fail to hear from the licensing agency.

Always Post Your Business License

Having a business license is a way of assuring customers that yours is a legal business. Your business license should be posted in a visible place at your business location. If you are exhibiting or selling at a trade show, you should (in fact, may be required to) have a copy on display. A copy of your business license may also be requested to establish accounts with vendors or to gain admission to trade and industry shows.

Sample

To give you an idea of some of the types of information that may be requested, a sample of a business license application can be seen on the next page. Applications will vary according to your city or county.

Sample Business License

CITY OF WESTMINSTER APPLICATION FOR BUSINESS, PROFESSION AND TRADE LICENSE

BUSINESS NAME	DATE	PROPERTY OWNER NAME
BUSINESS NAME (E)	BUSINESS PHONE	PHONE NUMBER
BUSINESS ADDRESS	OWNERSHIP	ALARM COMPANY NAME
MAILING ADDRESS	SOLE ☐ PARTNERSHIP ☐	PHONE NUMBER
TYPE OF BUSINESS	CORPORATION ☐	

FEDERAL EMPLOYER ID NO.	STATE EMPLOYER ID NO.	SALES TAX NUMBER	CONTRACTORS NO.

TAX _____ APPLICATION _____ PENALTY _____ TOTAL PAID _____ FICTITIOUS NAME NO. _____

BUSINESS OWNER(S) --- PARTNER(S) --- OFFICER(S)

HOME ADDRESS

CONFIDENTIAL

1
NAME_____ TITLE_____
STREET_____ PHONE_____
CITY_____ STATE _____ ZIP_____

DRIVERS LICENSE NUMBER

SOCIAL SECURITY NUMBER

2
NAME_____ TITLE_____
STREET_____ PHONE_____
CITY_____ STATE _____ ZIP_____

DRIVERS LICENSE NUMBER

SOCIAL SECURITY NUMBER

3
NAME_____ TITLE_____
STREET_____ PHONE_____
CITY_____ STATE _____ ZIP_____

DRIVERS LICENSE NUMBER

SOCIAL SECURITY NUMBER

I DECLARE UNDER PENALTY OF MAKING A FALSE CERTIFICATION THAT THE FOREGOING INFORMATION IS TRUE AND CORRECT TO THE BEST OF MY KNOWLEDGE AND BELIEF.

_____
OWNER, PARTNER, OFFICER

Registering a Fictitious Name (Filing a "DBA")

A fictitious name is commonly referred to as a DBA, which stands for "DOING BUSINESS AS." A fictitious name is any business name that does not contain your own name as a part of it. In some states, that means your legal name (frequently first and last).

❖ ❖ ❖ ❖

If you are not a corporation and you plan to conduct business under a fictitious name, you must file a DBA. If you are a corporation, ownership of your name is ensured when you incorporate. Also, if your legal name is considered very common, you may be required to file a DBA.

The following are examples to illustrate this point:

- ❖ Ocean Adventures: DBA required
- ❖ Glenn's Ocean Adventures: DBA required
- ❖ Sullivan's Ocean Adventures: DBA probably required
- ❖ Glenn Sullivan's Ocean Adventures: No DBA required
- ❖ John Smith's Ocean Adventures: DBA may be required (because name is common)
- ❖ Ocean Adventures, Inc.: No DBA required (corporation)

Filing your DBA is one of the first tasks to be undertaken because every other piece of paperwork requires the business name. Your bank will also require a copy of your DBA before they will open a business account under that name. This is the only authorization they have for depositing or cashing checks made out to that business name or written against its account.

Your business name should be free of conflict with names already registered in your area. Find out if a corporation has staked a claim to your name by calling your state's office of name availability. You may also wish to check the DBA books at the county clerk's office. Finding out at a later date that your name is already legally registered to another business will result in having to redo all of your paperwork.

 Note: You may wish to refer back to Chapter 4, "Choosing a Business Name," for further information on how to research the name of your business.

If You Fail to File

Registering a business name is very important for your own protection as well as for compliance with the law. Registration of that name gives you exclusive rights to it. It also keeps others from filing the same or a similar name and capitalizing on the hard work and investments you have made in your business.

Unfortunately, there are individuals who lurk in the shadows waiting for just such an opportunity. About eight years ago, we had a business owner in one of our classes who had built a very successful electronics firm. However, he failed to file a DBA. Someone else discovered his error, filed under his business name and offered him the option of either paying to buy the name back or ceasing to do business under that name. The business owner refused to pay the blackmail and chose to re-establish under a new name. The continuity of his business was set back and he lost a large amount of business trying to re-establish under the new name.

The time and money spent to file a DBA is very small compared to the benefits you will derive from becoming the legal owner of your business name.

How to File a DBA

Assuming you have chosen a fictitious name, it is time to register it (or file it) with the city or county in which you are doing business. This is a two-part process: (1) publishing your fictitious name through a general circulation newspaper and (2) filing that name with the county clerk.

1. *Publishing your fictitious name.* Your fictitious name must be published in a general circulation newspaper in the county your business is located in. It must appear in four consecutive editions.

When your fictitious name is published, the newspaper will send you a copy of the publication and issue a Publication Certificate. The fee for this service may vary from somewhere between $20 to $75.

2. *Filing with the county clerk.* The Publication Certificate has to be filed with the City or County Clerk. They will send you proof that it has been recorded. Fees for filing your DBA will vary, but generally run somewhere between $15 and $50.

Some newspapers will collect your fees *and* file for you after publishing. This will save you a trip to the County Clerk's office. Others will publish only and require that you do your own filing. As you can see above, there is also a lot of variation in the fees they charge for this service. Local newspapers frequently charge less and are easier to access. It would be wise for you to do some calling to various newspapers and ask the following questions:

✦ Do you publish new DBAs?

✦ What is your charge for the publication of a DBA?

✦ Do you (the newspaper) also file with the City or County Clerk? If so what are the fees for filing?

✦ What information do I need to bring with me in order to complete the Fictitious Name Statement?

Renewal of Your DBA

You will be required to renew your DBA at certain intervals — such as every five years. You will be notified by the filing agency when it is time to renew. Again, it is your responsibility to know when it must be done and to protect yourself by inquiring if you do not receive your renewal notification. Renewal does not require republishing, but will involve a fee to the City or County Clerk.

Alert: There are companies that keep track of expiring DBAs and send you official-looking notices to refile. They also build in a hidden fee. Refiling is very simple. Be sure your notice is the official one from the County Clerk.

Sample Forms

The next two pages contain samples of a **Fictitious Business Name Statement** and an example of a **Proof of Publication** that has been filed with the County Clerk's office.

Fictitious Business Name Statement
Sample Form

REMINDER
1. Submit original and 3 copies.
2. Filing fee $24.00 for one business name.
   $5.00 for each additional business name.
   $5.00 for each additional partner after first two.
3. **Provide return stamped envelope if mailed.**

☐ New Fictitious Business Name Statement

☐ Refile

GARY L. GRANVILLE, COUNTY CLERK
PUBLIC SERVICES DIVISION
211 W. SANTA ANA BOULEVARD
POST OFFICE BOX 22013
SANTA ANA, CA 92702-2013

THIS STATEMENT WAS FILED WITH THE COUNTY CLERK OF ORANGE COUNTY ON DATE INDICATED BY FILE STAMP BELOW.

FICTITIOUS BUSINESS NAME STATEMENT

File No. _____   THE FOLLOWING PERSON(S) IS (ARE) DOING BUSINESS AS: (TYPE ALL INFORMATION)

1. Fictitious Business Name(s)

2. Street Address, City & State of Principal place of Business in California   Zip Code

3. Full name of Registrant   (if corporation—show state of incorporation)

   Residence Address   City   State   Zip Code

   Full name of Registrant   (if corporation—show state of incorporation)

   Residence Address   City   State   Zip Code

   Full name of Registrant   (if corporation—show state of incorporation)

   Residence Address   City   State   Zip Code

4. (CHECK ONE ONLY) This business is conducted by ( ) an individual ( ) a general partnership ( ) a limited partnership ( ) an unincorporated association other than a partnership ( ) a corporation ( ) a business trust ( ) co-partners ( ) husband and wife ( ) joint venture ( ) other—please specify ( )

5. THE REGISTRANT(S) COMMENCED TO TRANSACT BUSINESS UNDER THE FICTITIOUS BUSINESS NAME(S) LISTED ABOVE ON:

   DATE:

   NOTICE: THIS FICTITIOUS NAME STATEMENT EXPIRES FIVE YEARS FROM THE DATE IT WAS FILED IN THE OFFICE OF THE COUNTY CLERK. A NEW FICTITIOUS BUSINESS NAME STATEMENT MUST BE FILED BEFORE THAT TIME. THE FILING OF THIS STATEMENT DOES NOT OF ITSELF AUTHORIZE THE USE IN THIS STATE OF A FICTITIOUS BUSINESS NAME IN VIOLATION OF THE RIGHTS OF ANOTHER UNDER FEDERAL, STATE, OR COMMON LAW (SEE SECTION 14400 ET SEQ., BUSINESS AND PROFESSIONS CODE).

6. Signature _____

   _____ (TYPE OR PRINT NAME)

   If Registrant is a corporation sign below:

   Corporation Name _____

   Signature & Title _____

Publication Certificate Sample

PROOF OF PUBLICATION
(2015.5c.c.p.)

STATE OF CALIFORNIA

COUNTY OF ORANGE

I am a citizen of the United States and a resident of the County aforesaid; I am over the age of eighteen years, and not a party to or interested in the above-entitled matter. I am the principal clerk of the printer of the the Orange Big News, a newspaper of general circulation printed and published weekly in the City of Orangetown, County of Orange, and which newspaper has been adjudged a newspaper of general circulation by the Superior Court of the County of Orange, State of California, under the date of April 14, 1977, Case Number A-62222, that the notice of which the annexed is a printed copy (set in type not smaller than nonpareil), has been published in each regular and entire issue of said newspaper and not in any supplement thereof on the following dates, to wit:

...........9/07 9/14 9/21 9/28..........

all in the year 19 96.

I certify (or declare) under penalty of perjury that the foregoing is true and correct.

Dated at Orangetown, California, this.....28th.......day

of.....September....................., 19....96....

Arlene S. Herzog
....
Signature

ORANGE BIG NEWS
533 W Harper
Orangetown, California 92622

OCH FORM NO. 0023-6/78-621-2M

This space is for the County Clerk's Filing Stamp

FILED

SEP 28 1996

PETER M. JONES, County Clerk

By_____DEPUTY

Proof of Publication of

FICTITIOUS BUSINESS NAME STATEMENT
F5987003

The following person(s) are doing business as:
Ace Sporting Goods
12345 Edwards St.
Anytown, CA 93456

1. JOHN R. SMITH
2345 Newstreet Drive
Anytown, CA 93456
This business is conducted by an individual.
The registrant commenced to transact business under the fictitious business name or names listed above on June 7, 1996.
Published: Orange Big News September 7, 14, 21, 28, 1996

PROOF OF PUBLICATION

F-_____

Obtaining a Seller's Permit

Anyone who purchases items for resale or who provides a taxable service must get a seller's permit number. This number is required in all states where sales tax is collected.

◆ ◆ ◆ ◆ ◆

Applying for a Seller's Permit

Information regarding sales tax and getting a seller's permit can be obtained through your state's Department of Revenue. Applications can be made through your local state offices. After filling out your application, you will be called in for an interview. Following this interview and a review of your application, it will be determined whether you qualify for a seller's permit. For this reason, it is imperative you understand exactly what you are requesting and the purpose for which you are requesting it. The wrong answer to a question can result in the denial of your certificate.

 Note: An application from the California State Board of Equalization is included as a sample for your information on page 110.

Purpose of a Seller's Permit

A sales tax is imposed upon retailers for the privilege of selling tangible personal property at retail within a state. The retailer, not the customer, is the person liable and responsible for paying the sales tax. Consequently, every seller engaged in the business of selling a tangible product or of providing a taxable service in a state where sales tax is collected is required to hold a seller's permit for the purpose of reporting and paying their sales and use tax liability. The seller's permit is more commonly referred to as a **resale tax number**.

Because of the complexity of the sales tax process, it may be difficult for you to determine which of your products and services will be taxable. You may request information sheets from the State Department of Revenue or your local State Board of Equalization that will explain the sales tax regulations on your particular type of business. You may also request a ruling to determine whether your product or service is taxable under a particular circumstance. Later, you must be sure to keep abreast of any changes that are made regarding the taxing of sales for your particular industry.

Your request must be on the basis that your business will be selling taxable items to your customers or that you will be providing a taxable service. Any other reason for your request will be grounds for denial. For example, many food services are not taxable unless they are provided at an event that charges admission. Therefore, a resale tax number would not be warranted.

Warning: *Do not use the word "buy" when you are applying for a seller's permit. Even though you may gain some purchasing advantages by having a seller's permit, this is not a valid reason for getting one. In fact, the mention of your intent to use it for the purchase of goods may prejudice the interviewer against you.*

State Laws Vary

The laws governing the collection of sales tax can be very complicated. Unfortunately, they also vary greatly from state to state. There have been many attempts to come up with a uniform sales tax system that would be fair to the consumer and at the same time guarantee collection of sales tax on all applicable sales. Individual states are also working to ensure that out-of-state companies servicing companies in-state and selling products through local outlets are collecting and reporting sales tax.

Misuse of Your Seller's Permit

Once you have been issued a resale tax number, it is imperative that you use it only for the purpose for which it was intended. Many tax numbers have been used to avoid paying sales tax on business-related purchases as well as tax on personal items. Purposeful misuse of a seller's permit has long been a laughing matter with many users. If you get caught, however, it may cease to be something to brag about. Most states are expanding their efforts to catch offenders. The penalties for misuse are very serious and may involve a heavy fine and/or a jail sentence.

The rule of thumb is: If you do not intend to resell your purchase through your business, do not use your resale number to buy tax free.

At this point, we feel that it is only fair to say that there is some validity to using your resale number to purchase wholesale. Many wholesalers do ask you to file a resale card with them before selling to you at wholesale prices. However, this does not exempt you from paying sales tax. It may only be a means of adding credibility as a business owner. In fact, if the seller does not collect from you at the time of the sale, you will be required to include the purchase in your periodic sales tax report and pay the sales tax at that time.

Resale Certificate

If you are purchasing goods for resale, the supplier or manufacturer will ask you to fill out a resale certificate to keep on file validating a sale to you on a tax-free basis. By the same token, when you sell to another dealer, you must also have the dealer fill out a resale card for your files. If the state later questions your nontaxable sales, you will have documentation as to why you did not collect tax on the sale. Pads of resale certificates may be purchased at almost any stationery supply store.

An example of a resale certificate can be found on page 111 at the end of this chapter.

Reporting Sales Tax

As previously stated, the purpose of a seller's permit is to provide the state with a means of collecting sales tax. To accomplish this, the sales tax must be accounted for by the final seller and sent to the state along with a report of the sources of those taxes. For this reason, the seller must keep accurate records as to the types of sales made and the amount of sales falling within each of the following categories:

- ◆ Gross sales
- ◆ Purchase price of property purchased without sales tax and used for purposes other than resale
- ◆ Sales to other retailers for purposes of resale
- ◆ Non-taxable sale of food products
- ◆ Non-taxable labor (repair and installation)
- ◆ Sales to the U.S. government

⊕ Sales in interstate or foreign commerce to out-of-state consumers

⊕ Bad debt losses on taxable sales

⊕ Other exempt transactions

 Note: Sales tax rates may vary from county to county. When you are selling out of your local area, you will collect sales tax based on the current rate in that area. You will also be required to keep an accurate record of those sales. In many cases a portion of your state's sales tax may be designated as belonging to a transit district, special assessment, etc. For instance, the State of California has many transit districts that are allocated one half of one percent to support their mass transportation systems. Therefore, a retailer from Los Angeles selling at a trade show in San Francisco will have to report the amount of those sales so the funds may be properly divided by the state agency.

The state will require you to file a quarterly report for summarizing your sales for the period. If your taxable sales are unusually small, you may only have to report annually. If they are excessive, you may be required to place a bond and report monthly. The reporting form will be sent to you by the Department of Revenue or State Board of Equalization. You must complete the report and mail it to the state, along with your check in the amount of sales tax due by a certain date (usually at the end of the month following the reported period).

 ## TECH TIP 13
Keeping Track of Sales for Easy Sales Tax Reporting

Sales tax reporting can be a long and tedious process—or you can do it at the click of a mouse! The secret is to utilize your accounting software to generate the information you need for your report to your local sales tax authority.

In order to generate the right information, you will have to think in terms of sales tax reporting when you set up your chart of accounts. This means that revenue accounts will need to be divided not only by the types of products and services you sell, but also according to their applicability to sales tax reporting.

Example: If you are in the business of selling two taxable products and your state requires sales information on (1) taxable sales, (2) out-of-state sales, (3) sales to resellers, and (4) sales tax payable, your chart of revenue accounts could be set up as follows:

Taxable Sales	Out-of State Sales	Reseller Sales
Product #1	Product #1	Product #1
Product #2	Product #2	Product #2

When sales revenue deposits are made, they are "split;" deposits and revenues are allocated among the appropriate accounts. Sales tax amounts will be automatically calculated on the taxable sales.

The Benefit: At any given time, you will be able to generate a report that will give you the numbers you need for your state's sales tax report.

Again a note of caution about responsibility for reporting: If you do not receive a report form in the mail, it will be your responsibility to call the Department of Revenue and request they send one to you.

When you receive this report, you will also receive a Tax Information Sheet with featured articles on sales tax regulations and crackdowns. Take the time to read it carefully, especially the information that may pertain to your particular industry. Failure to properly report may result in loss of your resale privilege as well as the more serious penalties mentioned above.

An example of a **California State Board of Equalization Report** is included at the end of this chapter (page 112) for your convenience. The return for your state will probably be very similar in form.

Sales Tax Flow Chart

In the event you are somewhat confused as to the progression of goods from the manufacturer to the consumer and final payment of taxes to the state by the seller, we have prepared a Sales Tax Flow Chart for you. Examination of the flow chart should help to eliminate some of the confusion. The chart will cover sales that are made under five separate circumstances.

Sales Tax Flow Chart

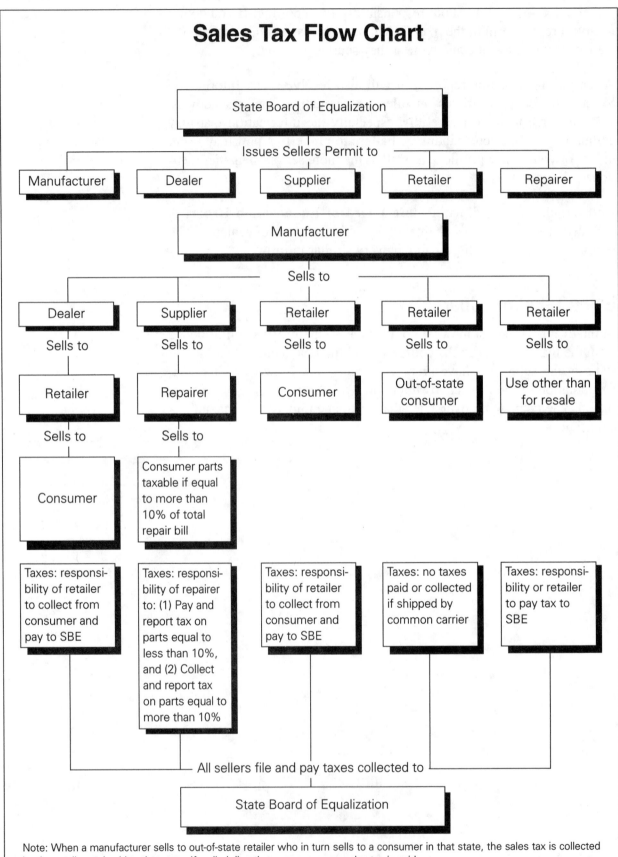

Note: When a manufacturer sells to out-of-state retailer who in turn sells to a consumer in that state, the sales tax is collected by the retailer and paid to that state. If mailed directly to consumer, no sales tax is paid.

Sample Application Seller's Permit

92-3   16,151

BT-400-MIP REV. 4 (10-91)
**APPLICATION FOR SELLER'S PERMIT AND
REGISTRATION AS A RETAILER
(INDIVIDUALS/PARTNERS)**

STATE OF CALIFORNIA
BOARD OF EQUALIZATION

Section I: Ownership Information

1. Please check type of ownership.
☐ Sole Owner ☐ Husband/Wife co-ownership ☐ Partnership

	FOR BOARD USE ONLY		
TAX	OFFICE	NUMBER	
S		—	

Business Code _____
Area Code _____
Preparer _____

Use additional sheet to include information about additional co-owners or partners

	Owner or Partner	Co-owner or partner
2. Full name (first, middle, last)		
3. Address (residence)		
4. Telephone (residence)	( )	( )
5. Social Security no.		
6. Driver's license no. Date of birth		
7. Present/past employer		
8. Name of spouse		
9. Social Security No. of spouse		
10. Driver's license no. of spouse		
11. Name, address and telephone number of two personal references	1. 2.	1. 2.
12. Signature		

Section II: Business Information

1. Business name	Business telephone ( )

2. Business address (Do not list P.O. Box or mailing service)	City	State	ZIP Code

3. Mailing address (if different from No. 2 above)	City	State	ZIP Code

4. Date you will begin sales			Days and hours of operation	Sun.	Mon.	Tue.	Wed.	Thurs.	Fri.	Sat.
Month	Day	Year								

5. Description of business
a. Type
☐ Retail ☐ Wholesale ☐ Manufacturing ☐ Repair ☐ Service ☐ Construction contractor

b. Activity
☐ Full-time ☐ Part-time ☐ Mail-order

c. Are you
☐ Starting a new business? ☐ Adding/dropping partner? ☐ Other?
☐ Buying a business?

d. Purchase price $ _____   Value of fixtures and equipment $ _____

If yes, please indicate name of former owner and account number _____

6. What will you sell?	6a. How many selling locations will you have? _____ (If 2 or more, please attach list of all locations.)

7. If alcoholic beverages are sold, please list your Alcoholic Beverage Control License number and type of license.

Continued on Reverse

Sample Application Seller's Permit

Page 2

16,151-2

92-3

BT-400-MIP (BACK) REV. 4 (10-91)

STATE OF CALIFORNIA
BOARD OF EQUALIZATION

	Address	Telephone ( )
8. Name of accountant/bookkeeper		
9. Name of business landlord	Address	Telephone ( )
10. Name of bank or other financial institution (checking and savings account)	Location	Account number

11. Name of major suppliers	Address	Products purchased

12. Other account numbers issued to you by the Board

Section III: Income and Expenses

1. Projected Monthly Business Expenses'	2. Projected Monthly Business Revenue	3. Information concerning Employment Development Department (EDD)
Rent $ _____	Total Gross Revenue $ _____	a. Are you registered with EDD? ☐ Yes ☐ No
Payroll $ _____	Non-taxable $ _____	b. If no, will your payroll exceed $100 per quarter? ☐ Yes ☐ No If yes, you must make application with EDD. Number of employees _____ See pamphlet DE 4525, "Employer Guide."
Misc. $ _____	Taxable $ _____	c. I have already received pamphlet DE 4525. ☐ Yes ☐ No
Total $ _____	Tax $ _____	d. I have already received pamphlet DE 44, "Employer's Withholding Guide." ☐ Yes ☐ No

Section IV: Certification

*The statements contained hereon are hereby certified to be correct to the best knowledge and belief
of the undersigned who is duly authorized to sign this application.*

SIGNATURE _____ TITLE _____

NAME (TYPED OR PRINTED) _____ DATE _____

FOR BOARD USE ONLY
Furnished to Applicant

REGULATIONS

Reporting Basis _____	☐ GA-324A	☐ REG. 1668	_____
Security Review ☐ BT-1009	☐ BT-400Y	☐ REG. 1698	_____
☐ BT-598 $ _____	☐ BT-467	☐ REG. 1700	_____
By _____	☐ BT-519	☐ DE-44	PAMPHLETS
Approved By _____	☐ BT-741	☐ DE-4525	_____
Remote Input Date _____	☐ BT-968	☐ _____	_____
By _____	☐ BT-1241C	☐ _____	RETURNS
Permit Issued ☐ Date _____			_____

Sample Resale Certificate

FIRM NAME _____

I HEREBY CERTIFY,
That I hold valid seller's permit No. _____
issued pursuant to the Sales and Use Tax Law; that I am engaged in the business of selling

_____

that the tangible personal property described herein which I shall purchase from:

_____

will be resold by me in the form of tangible personal property; PROVIDED however, that in the event any of such property is used for any purpose other than retention, demonstration, or display while holding it for sale in the regular course of business, it is understood that I am required by the Sales and Use Tax Law to report and pay for the tax, measured by the purchase price of such property.

Description of property to be purchased: _____

_____

Dated: _____   Signature: _____

at _____   By and Title: _____

Phone: _____   Address: _____

Sample State Board of Equalization Report

BT-401-A (S1F)
REV. 58 (10/92)

STATE OF
CALIFORNIA

BOARD OF EQUALIZATION

92712-2040

STATE, LOCAL & DISTRICT SALES & USE TAX RETURN

BOARD USE ONLY
RR - B/A
RR - QS
LOC
REG
ACC
REF

DUE ON OR BEFORE **JULY 31, 1993** FOR **APR THROUGH JUN 1993** 2-1993

Mail to: S R EA 23 2   0019   11/77   30022 037 0000
SR EA 24-   2

BOARD OF EQUALIZATION
P.O. BOX   942861
SACRAMENTO CA 94261-0001

If the above information is incorrect or your business has closed, please phone us at: **(714-558-4059)**

READ INSTRUCTIONS
BEFORE PREPARING

PLEASE ROUND
CENTS TO THE
NEAREST WHOLE
DOLLAR

1. TOTAL (GROSS) SALES	1.	$ .00
2. PURCHASES SUBJECT TO USE TAX	2.	.00
3. TOTAL (Line 1 plus Line 2)	3.	.00
4. SALES TO OTHER RETAILERS FOR PURPOSES OF RESALE	50 $	.00
5. NONTAXABLE SALES OF FOOD PRODUCTS	51	.00
6. NONTAXABLE LABOR (Repair and Installation)	52	.00
7. SALES TO THE UNITED STATES GOVERNMENT	53	.00
8. SALES IN INTERSTATE OR FOREIGN COMMERCE	54	.00
9. SALES TAX (IF ANY) INCLUDED ON LINE 1	55	.00
10. (a) BAD DEBT LOSSES ON TAXABLE SALES	56	.00
(b) COST OF TAX PAID PURCHASES RESOLD PRIOR TO USE	57	.00
(c) RETURNED TAXABLE MERCHANDISE	58	.00
(d) CASH DISCOUNTS ON TAXABLE SALES	59	.00
(e) OTHER (Clearly explain)	90	.00
11. TOTAL OF EXEMPT TRANSACTIONS REPORTED ON LINES 4 thru 10e (Add Lines 4 thru 10e)	11.	.00
12. TAXABLE TRANSACTIONS (Line 3 minus Line 11)	12.	.00
13. STATE & COUNTY TAX 6 1/4% (Multiply Amount on Line 12 by .0625)	13.	.00
14. ENTER AMOUNT FROM LINE 12	14.	.00
15. ADJUSTMENTS (See Instructions 15)	15.	.00
16. TAXABLE TRANSACTIONS (Line 14 plus or minus Line 15)	16.	.00
17. LOCAL TAX 1% (Multiply amount on Line 16 by .01)	17.	.00
18. DISTRICT TAX (From Schedule A Line A11) YOU MUST COMPLETE SCHEDULE A IF YOU ARE ENGAGED IN BUSINESS IN A TRANSACTIONS TAX DISTRICT	18.	.00
19. TOTAL STATE, COUNTY, LOCAL AND DISTRICT TAX (Total of Lines 13, 17, & 18)	19.	.00
20. DEDUCT sales or use tax imposed by other states and paid on the purchase price of tangible personal property. Purchase price must be included in Line 2	20.	.00
21. NET TAX (Line 19 minus Line 20)	21.	.00
22. Less PREPAYMENTS 1ST PREPAYMENT $ 2ND PREPAYMENT $ Total Prepayment	22.	$ .00
23. REMAINING TAX (Line 21 minus Line 22)	23.	.00
24. PENALTY of 10% is due if payment is made after due date shown above. Persons required to make payment by Electronic Funds Transfer may owe additional penalties (See Instruction 24)	24.	.00
25. INTEREST: One month's interest is due on tax for each month or fraction of a month that payment is delayed after the due date. The adjusted monthly interest rate is	0.8333 PERCENT (.008333) (10% DIVIDED BY 12) INTEREST 25.	.00
26. TOTAL AMOUNT DUE AND PAYABLE (Line 23 plus 24 & 25)	26.	$ .00

REC. NO.

PM

RE

I hereby certify that this return, including any accompanying schedules and statements, has been examined by me and to the best of my knowledge and belief is a true, correct and complete return.

SIGNATURE
AND TITLE _____ ( ) _____

MAKE CHECK OR MONEY ORDER PAYABLE TO STATE BOARD OF EQUALIZATION   PHONE NUMBER
Always Write Your Account Number on Your Check or Money Order

Setting Up a Bank Account

The selection of the bank you will do business with should be undertaken with a great deal of consideration. The banking industry changed drastically in the 1990s. There is a fast-paced move away from the single branch operation with its personal customer service and a move toward banking services via electronic communications. In most cases, you can no longer reach your local bank branch by telephone. If you have a problem, you will have to physically go into the bank or use your telephone to access information through an automated 800-customer service line. Automated deposits, online bill paying, and electronic transfers are becoming everyday processes.

❖ ❖ ❖ ❖ ❖

Choosing a Bank

Because new small businesses vary drastically in their needs and in the way they do business, it is most important that you determine what your current and future banking needs will be and select the bank that will be able to service those needs. If you are starting a small local service business and you have no plans to computerize, you will probably look for a smaller bank that offers more personalized service. If you are planning to start a business that will deal nationally or internationally, you will need a more aggressive bank that can provide you with the technology you need to effectively deal with your finances.

Things to Think about When You Choose Your Bank

The following will give you some basic information to think about when you are deciding which bank to select:

✦ *Have you already established a personal relationship with a banker?* If you already know the key management and personnel at your bank, you will have a head start when you need special consideration. Be aware, however, that first you must know that this bank can offer you the services you need.

✦ *What kind of loan programs are available through the bank?* Does this bank make business loans or does it confine itself to personal financing? Is the bank a participating SBA guaranteed lender? Does it participate in any other programs aimed at helping small business owners? Either now or sometime in the future you may need additional funds to operate or expand your business. It is easier to go to your own banker than to have to approach an unknown lender.

✦ *Does the bank offer merchant credit card services?* You may find that your business will be more profitable if you can offer VISA, MasterCard and/or American Express services to your customers. We are now living in an age where buyers of products and services do not carry cash and expect to pay with a credit card. The merchant now has the advantage of being able to instantly authorize the purchase and have funds deposited to the business account within 24 hours. The bank generally charges the merchant between three and four percent of the purchase amount for the service, but having the capability may significantly increase your sales.

Warning! If you are considering credit card services, do some careful planning before you commit your business to a program. You will get calls and e-mails from lot of companies wanting to set you up with merchant credit card services. Their salespeople are trained in the "fast sell." The costs to you can far outweigh the advantage gained by having the service. Ask for all the costs involved in setting up the service and the monthly charges for maintaining the service. Also determine the cost should you decide to discontinue services after a period of time. One company rented their terminal for $10 per month. However, if you quit in six months, you would owe $1,750 for the machine. The irony—the terminal costs only $200 to $300 to purchase (or $10 per month to rent) from most reputable banks. Also watch for non-refundable application fees and other miscellaneous charges, as well as restrictions on types of purchases you may accept (telephone orders, Internet orders, etc.).

✦ *What does the bank offer in the way of a business bank account?* Is there a holding period on your deposits? If so, can it be waived? Will there be a service charge to maintain your account? Is it an interest-bearing account? If so, do you have to maintain a minimum balance? What is the policy regarding returned checks from your customers? Does the bank offer overdraw protection? What other kinds of accounts does the bank have that will allow you to divert temporary funds where they can earn more and still stay liquid?

◈ *Is the bank a federal depository bank?* If your business has employees and you are paying any of those employees over a certain amount, you will have to deposit funds in a separate depository account on a regular basis. It will be more convenient if you can do all of your banking in the same place.

◈ *What additional services are available at the bank?* Do they have branches available in several locations? What days and hours are they open? Can you call your local branch if you have a problem? Do they have 24-hour ATM services? Do they have safe deposit boxes? Do they have notary services? Do they have merchant windows for expedited business banking services? What other services does the bank have that might be required by your business?

◈ *Does the bank provide electronic banking services?* With the new advances in computer technology, many banks now offer remote banking through online services. You can quickly access account information, transfer money, pay bills, and more—all with the convenience of your computer.

Note: It would be wise for you to spend some time telephoning banks and savings & loan institutions to gather information. At the end of this chapter (page 119), we have provided a worksheet, **Choosing a Bank**, that will help you to compare advantages and disadvantages of the financial institutions you are considering.

Separate Business and Personal Finances

Many times, a new business owner will be tempted to run business finances through personal accounts. **Do not mix** the two by trying to use the same checking account for your home and business. It is imperative that you keep your personal and business finances separate.

The IRS does not look kindly on a business that "co-mingles" personal and business moneys. The fate of more than one small business owner has been determined based on this issue during an audit—and generally not in the business' favor.

Mixing business and personal finances will also cause you many problems with your recordkeeping and tax computations. The recordkeeping process becomes very complicated and creates a confusing paper trail when you use business funds for personal obligations and vice versa.

Business accounts are necessary for credibility when dealing with other businesses. Many of your vendors will not accept a check unless it is preprinted with your business name and address. It may also be difficult, if not impossible, to establish an open account with a supplier or wholesaler if you do not have a business bank account.

Open a Checking Account

The first account you will need is a checking account. The following are some pointers that should help you to make needed decisions:

◈ *Your DBA is required.* If your business name is an assumed one, you cannot open a checking account under that name without first having filed a DBA as discussed earlier. The DBA is a means for giving the bank authority to deposit and cash checks under your fictitious name. It should be noted here, that banking policy at most financial institutions preclude offering interest-bearing checking accounts unless your name is part of the company name. If you have filed a DBA, be sure to take your receipt with you when you open your checking account. The bank will require a copy for their records.

◈ *Select a checkbook style.* When you open your checking account, you will be asked what style of checks you wish to order. You will have to decide between the book type and the wallet type. The smaller one is easier to carry, but the book type is the better choice. It will allow you to record more information about your checking transactions—information that can be invaluable during accounting procedures. There is a personal desk type checkbook that is smaller than the business size and still very adequate. You will have to ask about this particular style, as it is not included under business checkbook selections.

 Note: You do not have to order your checks from your bank. You can also order checks from office supply companies such as NEBS. The bank is the easiest source, but others may be less expensive or suit you better.

◈ *How many checks should you order?* Be sure to think ahead as to your needs before deciding on the number of checks to order. Reordering of checks can be costly. Start with a minimum order. In most cases there will be some change that needs to be made before long. You may get a new telephone number or decide to add or subtract a name.

At the same time you order, you may request that your checks be numbered beginning at a number higher than 101. Frequently, this request will be denied on new accounts. However, if you are successful, the use of higher-numbered checks may keep the recipients

TECH TIP 14
Computer Checks Save Time and Money

Many small businesses do their bookkeeping with a computer software program such as *QuickBooks*. These programs give you the option of printing your checks directly to computer check forms that are purchased from various office supply retailers. The accounting software also maintains the check register and copies of the checks you have written. If you regularly send checks to the same payee, the address will automatically be printed on the check in a position that will align with windowed envelopes, saving you the time required to address envelopes.

If you choose this alternative, you will have to supply the vender with your account number, bank number, bank name, etc. There are also computer programs that will allow you to design and print your own checks.

of your checks from being tipped off that you are a new business. You can always discard the first book or two books of checks and start your business with a higher check number. *If you generate your own computer checks, you can make your own decision and numbering is no problem.*

✦ *Arrange for overdraws.* It is best if you always maintain a healthy checking account balance for your business. However, there may be times when you have to make an unexpected purchase or you make an arithmetic error that will cause your account to be overdrawn. Providing coverage for these instances can save you time and embarrassment.

✦ *Get an ATM card for your account.* This will allow you to deposit or withdraw funds during non-banking hours. It will also allow you to access your funds at remote locations. It is now also becoming common for many businesses to directly accept your ATM card when you purchase products or services from them.

Additional Accounts You May Wish to Consider

In addition to your checking account, you may also wish to consider other types of accounts such as savings, money market, CDs, etc. The interest rates are the lowest on regular savings accounts. They are usually higher on money market, CD, and other special accounts. Some have limits and withdrawals before specified dates may impose penalties. Some are more liquid and a limited number of checks can be drawn on the account without penalty as long as you maintain a minimum balance. The earnings are usually proportionate to the length of time your funds are committed.

In Conclusion

Keep in mind that all accounts need not be at the same financial institution. However, it only makes sense that the amount of business you do with any one bank will be directly proportional to the benefits you will derive from it. Be sure to look at the stability of the bank you are considering. You will want to feel secure that tomorrow morning when you wake up your funds will still be available to you.

A good banking record, along with the establishment of rapport with management and personnel of your bank, may get you special concessions. For example, the hold on your deposits may be waived if the management so desires or notary services may be extended for free as a courtesy. If you already have a bank you have been satisfied with, you may wish to deal where you already have the advantage of being known by them as a valued customer.

Banking is serious business. Selection of the right bank and the right kinds of services will be a definite asset to your business.

Choosing a Bank Worksheet

	Name of Potential Financial Institution		
	A. City Bank	**B.** Home National Bank	**C.**
1. Have you already established a working relationship with: a. the management? b. the personnel?	Manager: J. Smith personnel: great	Manager: L. Jones (service-oriented) tellers: friendly	
2. What kind of business bank accounts are available?	business checking + CDs, etc.	business checking + CDs, etc.	
3. Does this bank offer merchant credit card services?	no	yes	
4. Does the business participate in business loan programs?	real estate only	preferred SBA lender	
5. Is the bank a federal depository bank?	yes	yes	
6. Is the bank a stable financial institution?	27-year-old	22-year-old	
7. How many branches does the bank have?	7	103	
8. Is the location of the bank convenient for your business?	yes	yes	
9. What are the bank's hours of operation? Are they open on Saturdays?	9-3 Mon-Thurs. 9-6 F; 10-1 Sat	9-3 Mon-Thurs. 9-6 F; 10-3 Sat	
10. Will the bank place a holding period on your deposits?	3 days	waived except for 2nd party	
11. What will it cost you to have a business checking account?	free w/$500 min.	free w/$750 min.	
12. What other services does the bank have: a. electronic banking? b. safe deposit? c. notary public? d. electronic transfer? e. other?	a. no b. yes (free) c. no d. yes e. ATM	a. yes b. yes c. yes d. yes e. ATM; seminars	
13. What is your overall feeling about the bank?	nice bank, but does not fill need	seems to be stable and fills all needs	

Selecting Your Insurance

· ·

At some point during the formation of a business, the question of insurance needs will necessarily arise. In fact, if you are writing a business plan, insurance will be one of the topics you cover in the Organizational Plan and interpret into costs in your Financial Documents.

❖ ❖ ❖ ❖ ❖

Today's world of rapidly-expanding technology goes hand-in-hand with a society steeped in lawsuits. The most innocent business owner can find himself/herself involved in legal actions against the business. In addition to liability, there are many other insurance considerations such as fire, flood, earthquake, theft, auto, worker's compensation, and health insurance that need to be addressed during the period of ownership.

The above are all concerns during the lifetime of the owner. What happens if the owner dies? There may be a need for life insurance and a buy-sell agreement to safeguard your beneficiaries.

Shopping for an Insurance Company

Shopping for an insurance company is like shopping for a bank. Careful research will help you to determine what company can best serve your needs and provide you with affordable coverage.

Call your current insurance company and see what they have to offer in the way of business insurance. Check with several other independent agents you know or that have

· · · · · ·

been recommended by your business associates. Ask them to discuss your business with you and recommend an insurance package that will give you the best coverage for the least number of dollars.

If your insurance needs are unique because of your type of business, you can look through your trade journals. Many times, business insurance companies will advertise in those journals, especially if the type of insurance they are advertising is not available with major companies. For example, food industries have their own unique considerations. Coverage is very expensive and they must usually seek a specialized insurance company.

What Are the Basic Kinds of Insurance?

As we stated before, there are many different kinds of insurance. In fact, there are so many kinds of insurance that most small business owners would go bankrupt if they were paying for the highest protection possible in all areas.

Most small businesses buy what is generally known as a Business Owner's Policy (BOP). The policy generally includes property, liability, criminal coverage, and various specialty coverage needed by the business. The advantage of a Business Owner's Policy is that it usually costs less than if each of the types of coverage were purchased separately.

In the following pages, we will address some of the most basic types of insurance that should be considered. There are two general categories under which all business insurance falls. They are "Property and Liability Insurance" and "Life and Health Insurance."

Property and Liability Insurance

Property insurance covers buildings and their contents against losses due to such things as fire, theft, wind, earthquake, flood, etc. Some of those risks may be specifically excluded in your policy and may require the purchase of additional policies (earthquake, flood, ground water, etc.).

Liability protects a business when it is sued for injury or property damage to third parties. This type of coverage pays damages related to bodily injury, property damage, and personal injury. These policies carry certain limits on the maximum that will be paid by an insurer for specific kinds of occurrences.

> ✦ *General liability.* Regular liability insurance pays for claims brought against your business because a customer or other person (the owner and employees are not covered) was injured on the business premises. It is wise to have this kind of liability insurance in

force when you open your business. It is not uncommon for a customer to fall and file a lawsuit that will be difficult for you to pay. Regular liability insurance also generally includes coverage for damage to property that you do not own or rent for your business (such as a water leak from your property that damages property in an adjoining business).

◆ *Property damage liability.* This policy covers damage to property that you lease or rent and property that belongs to your customers.

◆ *Fire insurance.* Protects your premises, fixed assets, and inventory against fire. Fire liability covers fire damage to property you are leasing or renting.

◆ *Earthquake insurance and flood insurance.* If you live in an area that has a likelihood of being damaged by an earthquake or some other serious act of nature, you may be wise to obtain special insurance coverage. The premiums are usually high, but well worth it if you are hit by a disaster.

◆ *Theft.* Protects against burglary and robbery at your place of business.

◆ *Fidelity bonds.* Protect a company against employee dishonesty.

◆ *Surety bonds.* Provides monetary compensation in the event a contractor fails to perform specific acts or complete work within the agreed-upon period of time.

◆ *Boiler and machinery coverage.* Covers equipment that is essential to the business (i.e., computer and telephone systems, production equipment, etc.).

◆ *Product liability.* Protects against claims filed by anyone using your product after it leaves your business. In most cases you will be liable even if your product has not been used correctly. The cost of product liability is generally in proportion to the volume of sales and the degree of hazard involved.

◆ *Workers' compensation.* Most states require an employer to provide insurance that covers all employees in case of disability or illness related to the workplace. You can call your insurance carrier to get workers' comp or contact the State Employment Department for information on state-operated insurance. Although this is insurance that will cover employees, it is paid in full by the employer. The amount charged for workers' comp varies according to the number of employees you have and also according to the degree of risk involved. If you are in a high-risk industry, the premiums can be very costly.

Workers' comp is one of the most controversial issues today. Due to a high rate of fraud and the trend toward stress claims, many employers have literally been forced out of business because of their inability to pay increasing insurance costs. Many businesses have instituted safety-in-the-workplace programs and intervention programs to cut down on claims. There is also an emphasis being placed on fraud detection. To relieve stress-related claims, legislation is pending that will place a percentage value that must be attributable to those claims.

◆ *Business interruption insurance.* Coverage can generally be added to your regular policy that will pay you an amount approximately equal to what you would have earned in the event you have to close your business while your premises are being rebuilt or repaired. You can also buy Overhead Insurance that will pay operating expenses during that time. There are also additional types of coverage that can be purchased to cover business operations under separate circumstances such as hospitalization.

◆ *Vehicle insurance.* Most states require you to carry a certain amount of liability coverage if you are going to operate a vehicle. Your regular insurance carrier will probably be able to insure your business vehicle. If you use the vehicle for both personal and business purposes, you will need to see that a rider is attached that will cover the business use. If you have employees that will be driving your business vehicles, be sure you have coverage that will be in effect in case of an accident.

◆ *Umbrella insurance.* This liability insurance can protect a business against catastrophic losses. It provides for extra protection for accidents involving a number of people. It also extends liability limits on auto policies (usually in increments of $1,000,000).

Life Insurance

One of the concerns of spouses and beneficiaries of a business owner is the question of what happens to that business if the owner dies. With the death of an owner comes responsibility of providing for the disposition of the business. You may need life insurance and some kind of a buy/sell agreement. If you die without having made necessary provisions, your beneficiaries may be forced to sell or dismantle the business to pay the estate taxes that might be due. If, instead, you have planned ahead and have an adequate life insurance policy, your beneficiaries can use the insurance proceeds to pay the estate taxes and allow the business to continue to operate. If they decide to sell the business, they will still be left with something to sell.

Life insurance can be an especially important consideration for a partnership. In many community-property states, if a partner dies, his or her spouse now owns that share of the business and has the authority to make that partner's decisions. This can create a situation that may be extremely unsatisfactory to either the surviving partner or the spouse. That is why it is important to have a partnership agreement that spells out what happens if one partner dies. A life insurance policy can be included as part of the partnership agreement with a provision designating that the policy payoff be used by the surviving partner to buy the deceased partner's share of the business.

The purchase of individual permanent life insurance by business owners can fund a deferred compensation program on a non-tax qualified basis allowing owners to set aside money for retirement or pay a death benefit to the surviving spouse. Key life insurance can also be purchased to cover key people whose death might affect the company's sales and profitability. A term policy would pay to help replace the loss of the person. A permanent key person life insurance policy would also accumulate cash value to help fund that person's retirement plan.

Health Insurance

Health insurance has long been the nemesis of the self-employed. The costs are often prohibitive and the coverage poor. Many group policies are available through trade associations and insurance companies specializing in small business, but most of the premiums are fairly high.

The best advice we can give is that you should explore every avenue and continue to get quotes on new coverage being made available. If you have the opportunity to keep purchasing health insurance through a previous employer, that may be your best avenue.

Employee Benefits

This is another issue requiring some important decisions if you are a small business owner. Your employees certainly need health insurance. However, the high cost of group health plans has made it almost impossible for small business owners to provide it for employees even if they wish to do so. And statistics indicate that costs continue to rise due to a number of factors such as complexity of treatment, unnecessary care, stress claims, and defensive medicine.

In spite of this, a CCH/Gallup survey of 1,000 small business owners revealed that 50 percent offered health insurance benefits to employees. If you need to attract employees with special skills or talents, you will have to compete with other employers to get them. That may mean that you will need to offer a health plan.

Small employers are not required to provide health plans except in Hawaii. Hawaii is the first state to require employers to provide health insurance to all full-time employees through an indemnity plan or an HMO.

In order to get away from paying employee benefits many companies, including major corporations, are hiring personnel through temporary agencies. There are both state and IRS rules that apply to nonemployee (or contract) services. Be aware of the fact that these restrictions exist and be sure that you are properly classifying your workers. Classifying an employee as contract services when he or she is actually an employee carries some heavy tax penalties.

Other Considerations

Insurance coverage is a complicated subject and cannot be covered adequately in the space we have allotted here. We are not in the insurance business and therefore do not wish to have you consider this as advice in regard to the insurance you should purchase or from whom you should purchase it.

The material covered in this chapter is for the purpose of acquainting you with some general information regarding types of insurance that you should consider.

See your insurance professional to determine what is available and what would be best for your business and for you. It would also be wise to consult with your tax planner, especially in the area of life insurance.

After You Have Your Information

When you have received information from several insurance companies regarding coverage and costs, you will have some last decisions to make. You will have to look at your insurance needs in terms of immediate needs and long-term protection. Know what is required by the federal and state government, by your lender, or the title holder of your vehicles, etc. Also decide what kinds of insurance you will need to protect your business. Divide your insurance needs down into those that are required, necessary, and desirable. Decide what you can purchase now, what you will purchase when financing allows, and what you will put on hold until a future time.

To help you with your shopping. We have provided a worksheet on the next page that will help you when you are comparing insurance companies for coverage and costs. There is also an **Insurance Update Form** in the "Worksheets" section for your use.

Insurance Fact Sheet

I. Types of Business Insurance

Property and Liability
General liability
Property damage liability
Fire insurance
Earthquake/flood insurance
Theft
Fidelity bonds
Surety bonds
Boiler and machinery coverage
Product liability
Workers' compensation
Business interruption insurance
Vehicle insurance
Umbrella insurance

Life and Health
Life insurance
Disability insurance
Employee benefits
Group insurance
Retirement programs
Overhead expenses

II. Figure Out Your Insurance Priority Shopping List

Immediate protection that is: 1. Required _____

2. Necessary _____

3. Desirable _____

Long-term protection that is: 1. Required _____

2. Necessary _____

3. Desirable _____

III. Key Points

- Insurance is and should be a major factor to consider in forming a business.
- First year property and liability premiums will sometimes be higher than other years due to frequency of misstatement by the insured and high risk to the insurance company.
- Choosing your insurance agent/broker (consultant and buyer) is one of the most important decisions you can make.

IV. Five Steps to Prevent Your Business from Failing Due to an "Insurable" Cause

- Recognize risks you will be facing.
- Follow guidelines for covering them economically.
- Have a plan in mind.
- Get advice from experts.
- Do it now!

Financing Your Business

When you are planning to open a new business (or expand your current operation), four very important questions arise relating to finance:

1. Will you need to borrow money?
2. If you need outside financing, how much do you need and when will you need it?
3. What are the sources of funding available to meet your needs?
4. How much will it cost?

In order to make an intelligent decision on a timely basis, you will have to address all four of these questions. If you fail to do so, the lack of sufficient and ready capital can quickly lead to business failure.

❖ ❖ ❖ ❖ ❖

Will You Need to Borrow Money?

The first step is to ask yourself some questions that will help you to make the right decision—questions to help you realistically understand your financial needs and keep you from making costly errors that may ultimately bankrupt a potentially viable business. To determine whether you will need outside financing, some of the questions you might ask yourself are:

❖ Have I written a business plan so I can make financial decisions based on achieving the desired goals for my business? If you haven't written one, do so.

◈ Would I be willing to risk my own money on my venture? What are the risks? What are my own sources of available capital? If you are not willing to take a risk, don't expect someone else to.

◈ Do I really need additional financing or do I just need to manage my present cash flow more effectively?

◈ What do I need the money for? If I borrow, can I realistically project increased revenues? If so, when will those increased revenues justify the debt?

How Much Do You Need and When Do You Need It?

If you have decided you will need additional financing, then carefully assess what you want the money for and determine not only the amount, but also when you will need it. Many business owners overestimate or underestimate their capital requirements and/or do not time their financing to the best advantage. Either can lead to serious problems.

The first thing you need is a realistic *business plan* and one you intend to follow as closely as possible. (Does this sound repetitious?) The only way to look at every aspect of your business is through the planning process. It will force you to create an organizational plan, a marketing plan, and to quantify your concepts through the development of projected financial statements whose numbers can then be analyzed and used in the decision-making process. The projections give you an educated estimate of your financial needs and tell you when they will most likely occur. Your business plan will answer such questions as:

◈ What are my most critical needs?

◈ If I need the money for immediate operating capital, how much will I need to operate my business until it becomes self-sustaining?

◈ If I need the money to buy fixed assets for my business, has my research shown that I can reach the target market that will justify the purchase of those assets? If not now, when would be the optimum time to add those assets?

◈ If I need the money for marketing, what are the most effective ways to reach my target market? How much will it cost to advertise? Will the increased marketing be reflected in even higher increases in revenues? According to my industry trends, what are the best selling periods and when will I need financing in order to have the lead-time to advertise for the best results?

What Are the Sources Available to You?

Sources of financing available to prospective and expanding businesses falls into two broad categories. They are:

1. Debt financing (dollars borrowed)
2. Equity financing (ownership dollars injected into the business)

Debt Financing

Debt financing is generally obtained from one of two sources. It can come from either a non-professional source such as a friend, relative, customer, or colleague or from a traditional lending institution such as a bank, commercial finance company, or the U.S. Small Business Administration.

◈ *Friends or relatives.* Borrowing from a friend or relative is generally the most readily available source, especially when the capital requirements are smaller. This is frequently the least costly in terms of dollars, but may become the most costly in terms of personal relations if your repayment schedule is not timely or your venture does not work out. This avenue should be approached with great caution!

◈ *Angel programs.* For smaller business owners, women, and minorities, there has been a growing trend toward the development of "angel" programs through business organizations and companies specializing in small business. Individuals and small companies that want to invest smaller amounts of money in promising businesses are linked with those companies and the two decide whether the loan will be made. This avenue is still relatively new, but holds even more promise for the future.

◈ *Traditional lending institutions.* Banks, savings and loans, and commercial finance companies have long been the major sources of business financing, principally as short-term lenders offering demand loans, seasonal lines of credit, and single-purpose loans for fixed assets.

You should be aware of the fact that almost all lending institutions are strict about collateral requirements and they may require established businesses to provide one-third of the equity injection and start-ups up to 50 percent or more. Again, as a borrower, you will need to have a business plan with adequate documentation demonstrating a projected operating cash flow that will enable you to repay (on time) the loan with interest.

◈ *SBA guaranteed loans.* The SBA guaranteed loan program is a secondary source of financing. This option comes into play after private lending options have been denied. The SBA offers a variety of loan programs to eligible small businesses that cannot borrow on reasonable terms from conventional lenders in the amount needed without governmental help. Most of the SBAs business loans are made by private lenders and then guaranteed by the Agency. Though it may not necessarily be easier to be approved for an SBA guaranteed loan, the guaranty will allow you to obtain a loan with a longer maturity at better repayment terms and interest rates, thereby reducing your monthly payments and the initial loan burden. Visit the SBAs Web site for complete up-to-date information on their loan programs: www.sbaonline.sba.gov/financing/.

- **7(a) Guaranteed loan program.** This is the SBAs primary loan program. You can use a 7(a) loan to expand or renovate facilities; purchase machinery, equipment, fixtures; for leasehold improvements; to finance receivables and augment working capital; to refinance existing debt (with compelling reason); finance seasonal lines of credit; construct commercial buildings; and/or purchase land or buildings.

  Currently the maximum amount for a loan guaranty is $750,000. Loan amounts of $100,000 or less receive 80 percent of guaranty. All other loans receive a 75 percent SBA guaranty. The average size loan is $175,000 with an eight-year maturity. The 7(a) loan program is available to businesses that operate for profit and qualify as small under SBA size standard criteria.

  You submit a loan application to a lender for initial review. If the lender approves the loan subject to a SBA guaranty, a copy of the application and a credit analysis are forwarded by the lender to the nearest SBA office.

  The SBA looks for: good character, management expertise, financial resources to operate the business, feasible business plan, adequate equity or investment in the business, sufficient collateral, and the ability to repay the loan on time from the projected operating cash flow.

  After SBA approval, the lending institution closes the loan and disburses the funds; you make monthly loan payments directly to the lender. As with any loan, you are responsible for repaying the full amount of the loan.

  Generally liens will be taken on assets financed by SBA proceeds and the personal guarantee of the principal owners and/or the CEO are required. The borrower must pledge sufficient assets, to the extent that they are reasonably available, to adequately secure the loan. However, in most cases the SBA will not decline a loan where insufficient collateral is the only unfavorable factor. The lender sets the rate of interest: loans under seven years, max. prime +2.25 percent; seven years or more, max. 2.75 percent over prime; under $50,000, rates may be slightly higher.

- **CAPLines.** Eligibility and interest rate rules are the same as for 7(a) guaranteed loans. CAPLines is for the financing of assets. The primary collateral will be the short-term assets financed by the loan. SBA will guarantee 75 percent of up to $750,000 (80 percent on loans of $100,000 or less. There are five short-term working-capital loan programs for small businesses under CAPLines: (1) seasonal line; (2) contract line; (3) builders line; (4) standard asset-based line; and (5) small asset-based line. The asset-based lines must revolve.

- **International trade loan program.** Applicants must establish either that the loan proceeds will significantly expand existing export markets or develop new ones, or that the applicant is adversely affected by import competition. SBA can guaranty 75 percent of an amount up to $1,250,000 in combined working capital and fixed-asset loans. The lender must take a first-lien position on items financed. Only collateral located in the U.S., its territories, and possessions are acceptable as collateral under this program. Additional collateral may be required including personal guaranties, subordinate liens, or items that are not financed by the loan proceeds. The proceeds of the loan may not be used for debt repayment. Fees and interest rates are the same as for 7(a) loans.

- **Export working capital program.** This program is for exporters seeking short-term working capital. SBA will guarantee 90 percent of the principal and interest, up to $750,000. The EWCP uses a one-page application form and streamlined documentation, and turnaround is usually within ten days. You may also apply for a letter of prequalification from the SBA. Businesses must have operated for the past 12 months, not necessarily in exporting, prior to filing an application. The SBA does not regulate interest rates and the lender is not limited to the rates specified for regular 7(a) loans.

- **Defense loan and technical assistance (DELTA) program.** The DELTA Program is available to help defense-dependent small business concerns adversely affected by defense cuts to diversify into the commercial market. The Program provides both financial and technical assistance. A joint effort of the SBA and the Department of Defense, DELTA offers about $1 billion in gross lending authority. At least 25 percent of the business' revenues from the immediate preceding year must have come from defense-related contracts and the borrower must be able to create or retain one job per $35,000 of SBA assistance. Loan amounts are up to $1,250,000. The SBA processes, guarantees, and services DELTA loans through the regulations, forms, and operating criteria of the 7(a) program and the 504 Certified Development Company Program. Technical assistance is provided through SBDCs, SCORE, other federal agencies, and other technical and management assistance providers.

◆ *Streamlined applications and approvals.* There are several options available to lenders that help streamline delivery of the SBAs guaranty.

- **LowDoc loan program.** LowDoc is one of the SBAs most popular programs. Once you have met your lender's requirements for credit, LowDoc offers a simple, one-page SBA application form and rapid turnaround for loans of $100,000 or less. SBA will guarantee up to 80 percent of the loan amount. The loans should be adequately secured. Business assets are usually pledged and personal guarantees of the principals are required. The applicant completes the front of a one-page SBA application; the lender completes the back. The lender requires additional information. The same interest rate rules apply as in the 7(a) Program. To be eligible, business must have average annual sales for the past three years not exceeding $5 million and must have fewer than 100 employees. Business start-ups are also eligible for the LowDoc loan program.

- **FA$TRAK loan program.** This program makes capital available to businesses seeking loans of up to $100,000 without requiring the lender to use the SBA process. Lenders use their existing documentation and procedures to make and service loans. The SBA guarantees up to 50 percent of a FA$TRAK loan. Your local SBA office can provide you with a list of FA$TRAK lenders.

- **Certified and preferred lenders program.** The most active and expert SBA lenders qualify for the SBA's Certified and Preferred Lenders Program. Participants are delegated partial or full authority to approve loans, which results in faster service. Certified lenders are those that have been heavily involved in regular SBA loan-guaranty processing and have met certain other criteria. Preferred lenders are chosen from among the SBAs best lenders and enjoy full delegation of lending authority. A list of participants in the Certified and Preferred Lenders Program may be obtained from your local SBA office.

- **7(M) MicroLoan program.** The MicroLoan program provides small loans ranging from under $100 to $25,000. Under this program, the SBA makes funds available to nonprofit intermediaries; these, in turn, make the loans. The average loan size is $10,000. An intermediary usually processes completed applications in less than one week. This is a pilot program available at a limited number of locations. Microloans may be used to finance machinery, equipment, fixtures, and leasehold improvements. They may also be used to finance receivables and for working capital. They may not be used to pay existing debt. Depending on the earnings of your business, you may take up to six years to repay a microloan. Rates are pegged at no more than four percent over the prime rate. There is no guaranty fee. Each nonprofit lending organization will have its own collateral requirements, but must take as collateral any assets purchased with the microloan. Generally the personal guaranties of the business owners are also required.

- **504 Certified Development Company.** CDCs are nonprofit corporations set up to contribute to the economic development of their communities or regions. They work with the SBA and private-sector lenders to provide financing to small businesses. The program is designed to enable small businesses to create and retain jobs; the CDCs portfolio must create or retain one job for every $35,000 of debenture proceeds provided by the SBA. They provide small businesses with 10 or 20 year financing for the acquisition of land and buildings, machinery and equipment, or for constructing, modernizing, renovating, or converting existing facilities. To be eligible, the business must operate for profit. Tangible net worth must not exceed $6 million and average net income must not exceed $2 million for the past two years. The maximum loan amount is generally $750,000. The amount may go up to $1 million if the project meets public policy goals (i.e., business district revitalization, expansion of export, expansion of minority business). Collateral may include a mortgage on the land and the building being financed. Personal

TECH TIP 15
Y2K Action Loans Address the Year 2000 Computer Problems

On April 2, 1999 a new law went into effect requiring the U.S. Small Business Administration to provide a loan guaranty program to address the Year 2000 computer problems of small business concerns. This program utilizes current 7(a) policies and procedures, provides maximum flexibility in establishing terms and conditions of the loan, allows up to a one-year moratorium on principal payments, and provides that any reasonable doubts regarding ability to repay the debt be resolved in favor of the applicant.

Eligibility. Any borrower currently eligible under 7(a) can utilize this program.

Use of proceeds. Loan proceeds can be used only to address the Year 2000 computer problems including:

- the repair and acquisition of information technology systems.
- the purchase and repair of software.
- the purchase of consulting and other third party services, and related expenses.

- relief from substantial economic injury incurred as a direct result of the Year 2000 computer problems or as an indirect result caused by any other entity such as a service provider or supplier, if such economic injury is not compensated for by insurance or otherwise, after January 1, 2000.

Guaranty. Y2K loans are made by authorized SBA lenders and guaranteed by the SBA. SBA can provide up to a 90 percent guarantee on Y2K loans of $100,000 or less and up to 85 percent on Y2K loans of over $1,000,000.

For more information. The SBA has offices located throughout the United States. For one nearest you, look under U.S. government in your telephone directory, or call the SBA Answer Desk at 1-800-U-ASK-SBA. E-mail questions or comments can be directed to Greg Diercks, at: gregory.diercks@sba.gov

guarantees of principals are required. SBA will take business assets as collateral. Interest is set at second TD rate based on the current market rate for five and ten year U.S. Treasury Bonds and is generally below market rate.

Equity Financing

If your company has a high percentage of debt to equity (what you owe compared to what you own), you will find it difficult to get debt financing and will probably need to seek equity investment for additional funds. What this means simply is that you will trade a certain percentage of your company for a specific amount of money to be injected into the company.

Source of equity financing. As with debt capital, this type of capital can come from friends and relatives, from SBA-licensed investment companies, or from professional investors known as a *"venture capitalists."*

- ◈ *Friends and relatives.* Again, be reminded that mixing your friends or relatives and your business may not be a good idea.

- ◈ *SBA-licensed investment companies.* The SBA also licenses Small Business Investment Companies (SBICs). They make venture/risk investments by supplying equity capital and extending unsecured loans to small enterprises that meet their criteria. The SBIC program provides an alternative to bank financing, filling the gap between the availability of venture capital and the needs of small businesses that are either starting or growing. They use their own funds plus funds obtained at favorable rates with SBA guaranties and/or by selling their preferred stock to the SBA. SBICs are for-profit firms whose incentive is to share in the success of a small business. The program provides funding to all types of manufacturing and service industries.

- ◈ *Special considerations relating to venture capital.* The venture capitalist is a risk taker, usually specializing in related industries and preferring three- to five-year-old companies that have shown high growth potential and will offer higher-than-average profits to their shareholders. These investments are often arranged through venture capital firms that act as "matchmakers."

As risk takers, venture capitalists have a right to participate in the management of the business. If the company does not perform, they may become active in the decision-making process. The most frequent question we get asked is, *"What is the standard amount of equity you have to trade for financing?"* The trade of equity for capital is based on supply and demand. In other words, the deal is made according to who has the best bargaining power.

Venture capitalists also require the inclusion of an *exit strategy* in the company's business plan. The exit strategy lays out the future goals for the company and minimizes risk to the investor by providing a way out if there is a strong indicator that the business will fail to reach its profitability goals.

How Much Will It Cost?

The cost of financing is usually related to the degree of risk involved. If the risk is high, so is the cost.

- ◆ *The least expensive money to use is your own.* The cost to you is whatever you would have made on your money by investing it in other sources (savings, money market accounts, bonds, retirement plans, real estate, etc.).

  Note: At this point, we need to mention credit cards. Many new business owners borrow heavily on their credit cards only to find themselves in hock up to their ears. Credit cards are one of the most expensive sources of cash and have paved the road to bankruptcy court more than once. Don't get caught in this trap!

- ◆ *Friends and relatives.* The next lowest in cost generally comes from friends and relatives who may charge you a lower interest rate. But don't forget that it may cost you in other ways.

- ◆ *Banks and other traditional lenders.* The third on the cost ladder is probably the traditional lender (banks, SBA, etc.). This lender will want to know what the capital will be used for and will require that it be used for those specific needs. If the risk is too high, most conventional lenders cannot approve your loan because it would be a poor financial decision for the bank's investors. One default out of ten will undermine their whole program.

- ◆ *Outside lenders and venture capitalists.* Traditionally, the most expensive is the outside lender who charges a high interest rate because of the risk involved and the venture capitalist that requires a percentage of your business.

Calculating the Cost

Before you get a loan, take time to understand the terms under which the loan will be made. What is the interest rate? How long do you have to repay the loan? When will payments begin and how much will they be? What are you putting up as collateral? If you have venture capital injected into the business, what will be the overall price to you for the equity and control that you will forfeit?

Any source of financing can and should be calculated as to cost before the financing is finalized. Again back to your business plan. Determine when the financing is needed, plug-in cash injection, repayment figures, and resulting income projections into your cash flow statement and checkout the result. Will the financing make you more profitable and enable you to repay the lender or distribute profits to the venture capitalist?

In Summary

Securing financing for your company must be planned well in advance. The more immediate your need, the less likely you are to get the best terms. Don't ask your banker to give you a loan yesterday—and don't expect a venture capitalist to jump on the bandwagon because you suddenly need their money. Planning ahead for cash flow is one of the best means for determining if and when you will need a lender or investor. It will also help you to determine how much you need.

When you plan for financing, remember you will have to show that your industry has good potential for profit, and you also will have to present a strong case for the ability to manage your company through the period of debt. Getting financing is serious business for both you and for the lender/investor. *Take time to plan carefully for your financial needs and your company will prosper and grow accordingly.*

Keeping Your Books

It is not the purpose of this book to give you a course in small business accounting. However, we will attempt in the next few pages to acquaint you with the basic records you will need to keep. For a more comprehensive guide, we have a book entitled, *Keeping the Books: Basic Recordkeeping and Accounting for the Small Business* (Chicago: Dearborn, 1998). You also can take classes through most community colleges and the IRS gives small business tax classes at various locations on a regular basis. We also urge an alliance with a reputable tax professional to help you work out your accounting procedures.

✦ ✦ ✦ ✦ ✦

The Importance of Recordkeeping

Recordkeeping has two main functions:

1. To provide you with tax information that can be easily retrieved and verified. Poor recordkeeping can cause you a multitude of problems and may result in audits, penalties, and even the termination of your business.

2. To provide you with information that you can use to analyze your business. Accurate financial statements will help you to see trends and implement changes during the life of your business.

The keeping of accurate records is imperative if your business is to succeed. To be the most effective, you should set up a system that is as simple as possible and yet complete enough to give you any information that will be helpful in your business. If you have an

TECH TIP 16
Accounting Software

If you have a computer (as most people now do), you will be able to effectively utilize it to do your small business accounting.

The use of accounting software is only beneficial if: (1) you first have a good working knowledge of recordkeeping principles, and (2) you have developed reasonable skills when it comes to the operation of your computer. Even the most simple accounting software will require you to make decisions and adapt the setup to your own particular accounting needs.

QuickBooks Pro (not Quicken), by Intuit, is one of the software programs that does a good job of tracking business finances. There are also some other well-known accounting packages such as: One-Write Plus, Dac Easy, MYOB (Mind Your Own Business), and Peach Tree. Most of these packages are very reasonably-priced—many under $100 depending on how many modules are attached.

Once you set it up for your business and develop a chart of accounts, you can use it for all of your bookkeeping. The program will allow you to do as much or as little as you wish. For instance, you can choose whether or not to generate invoices and/or write checks from within the software. At any time, you can generate reports (P&Ls, balance sheet, customer accounts, etc.) for the time period of your choosing. This will enable you to look at your business at any time and to utilize the reports as analysis tools on which you can make decisions and implement changes. At the end of the year, if you have kept your bookkeeping up-to-date, it will also enable you to generate, at a click of your mouse, an annual profit & loss statement and balance sheet to take to your tax accountant.

Note: It would be wise to have the accounting professional that will handle your annual income tax returns help you to do the initial set-up of your software. He or she can recommend the software that will work best for you and maybe get you started by helping to setup your business, develop a chart of accounts, and learn how to handle issues (such as sales tax) that may require a more advanced understanding of the software.

accurate set of records, it will be possible for you to tell at a glance what is happening with your business—which areas are productive and cost-effective and which will require change.

Should You Hire an Accounting Professional?

If you will involve yourself in your bookkeeping as much as possible, you will be doubly aware of what is going on in your business. If your business is very small, we suggest you set-up a hands-on system and maintain most of your own general records throughout the year. If you are computer-literate (or brave enough to tackle the project), get one of the accounting software packages we mentioned previously.

Because there are very few business owners who are knowledgeable about all the fine points and changes in tax laws, it is best to delegate some jobs to an accounting professional. He or she can help you to initially develop a

Bookkeeping: the process of recording business transactions into the accounting records. The "books" are the documents in which the records of transactions are kept.

chart of accounts and set-up your books using coordinating software for easy transfer of information. Your tax professional can also maintain difficult records such as payroll and depreciation. You will want that same specialist to maximize your tax benefits by preparing your tax return at the end of the year.

If you would feel more comfortable having an accounting professional do all of your bookkeeping, you will still be wise to educate yourself about the basics. Ask your accountant to prepare a balance sheet and a profit & loss statement at the close of every month and be sure you will be able to read and understand them. The information on these two financial statements is essential to the effective running of your business.

Depreciation: a decrease in value through age, wear, or deterioration; a normal expense of doing business. There are laws and regulations governing the manner and time periods that may be used for depreciation.

When Do You Begin?

If you are reading this book, you are thinking about going into business or you have already begun your business. So now is the time to begin keeping records. All of the expenses you incur in start-up will be valid costs of doing business. Conversely, any revenues you generate must also be accounted for.

You can start by keeping a journal of your daily activities: where you go, who you see, what you spend. Keep track of business classes, mileage, supplies purchased, telephone calls, professional materials—everything that might relate to your business.

What Records Do You Need to Keep?

Your bookkeeping system must be tailored to your individual needs. Because no two businesses will have exactly the same concerns, it is best that you do not buy a ready-made set of books. Familiarize yourself with the information you will need and set up your records accordingly. As a business owner, you will be required to keep track of all of your income and expenses.

Again, simplicity is the key to small business accounting. There are many different types of general accounting records. Their purpose is to record each transaction that takes place in your business. The general records are then used to develop monthly and yearly financial statements to be used for tax reporting and financial analysis. You should set up only those general records you will need to document the information for your particular business. For instance, a car wash that does only cash business would not need "accounts receivable" records. Fewer records are easier to read and they will require less bookkeeping time.

General Records

Every business will require certain records to keep track of its daily transactions. These records are used to generate your monthly profit & loss statements and balance sheets. You should set up a recordkeeping schedule and keep your records current.

To acquaint you with the most common general records, we will define each one, provide you with a filled-in example at the back of the chapter and give you a blank form in the Appendix for you to copy and use for your own business.

◆ *Revenue & Expense Journal.* This is the main general record used by a business. It's used to record individual transactions where income is received and checks are written by your business. The transactions are recorded as revenues (monies for sales and interest earned) and expenses (checks written to pay for products and services received by you). At the end of the month, the columns in the Revenue & Expense journal are totaled. The totals are then transferred to that month's Profit & Loss statement. The new month begins with all revenue and expense categories at zero. See page 148 for an example of a **Revenue & Expense Journal**.

◆ *Petty Cash Record.* Petty cash refers to all of the purchases made with cash or personal checks when it is not convenient to pay with a business check. These transactions are recorded in a separate journal and paid by periodically writing a business check made out to "Petty Cash" that is recorded as an expense in the Revenue & Expense Journal and as a deposit in the Petty Cash Record. Petty cash transactions require careful recording. See page 149.

◆ *Inventory Records.* These are records that keep track of all products purchased or manufactured for resale. The IRS requires a beginning and ending inventory for each taxable year. Inventory control is a major factor contributing toward business success—or business failure. Internal use of these records will greatly enhance your profits. See pages 150–151.

◆ *Fixed Assets Log.* This is a list of all assets (tangible and intangible) that will have to be capitalized (or depreciated over a specified number of years). They are items purchased for use in your business (not resale), usually at a cost of $100 or more and not debited to an expense account. They are depreciated over a period determined by tax regulations. Examples might be as follows: buildings, vehicles, office equipment, production equipment, or office furniture. Land does not depreciate. Depreciation can be difficult to calculate because of the many IRS regulations that must be applied. It is best to let your tax preparer figure out your depreciation at the end of the year. See page 152.

♦ *Accounts Payable.* This is a record of debts owed by your company for goods purchased or services rendered to you in the pursuit of your business. You will need an efficient system for keeping track of what you owe and when it should be paid to get the best terms. If you are going to have a good credit record, the payment of these invoices must be timely. If you do not accumulate unpaid invoices, you may be able to dispense with this record. See page 153.

♦ *Accounts Receivable.* This record is used to keep track of debts owed to you by your customers as a result of the sale of products or the rendering of services. Each client with an open account should have a separate page with account information. Statements of balances due are sent to your account holders at the close of each month. If you do not have open accounts, you will also be able to dispense with this record. See page 154.

♦ *Mileage, Entertainment, and Travel Records.* These are the records used to keep track of auto and transportation expenses, meals, and entertainment of clients and travel out of your local area. Due to past abuse in these areas, the IRS requires careful documentation as proof that deductions claimed are in fact business-related expenses. We strongly suggest you organize a travel log, trip records, and entertainment records so they can be carried with you. It is much easier to keep track of them at the time they occur than to try to remember them and find receipts after the fact. In addition, keep all of your receipts. You can read more about "Travel and Entertainment" in IRS Publication #334, *Tax Guide for Small Business*. There are also separate IRS publications containing more detailed information. See pages 155–157.

♦ *Payroll Records.* The IRS has strict regulations regarding withholding and payroll taxes and their reporting. Payroll records are not easy to keep, even with a payroll software program. Leave these records to a trained tax expert. You will be informed what checks to write and these will be recorded in the Revenue & Expense Journal. The accounting professional will do all the tax reporting for you.

♦ *Business Checkbook.* Your checkbook is not only the means to pay your bills. It also serves as a record of who was paid, how much was paid, and what was purchased. Deposits are recorded and a balance of cash available is always at your fingertips. It is best to use a desk-sized checkbook with plenty of space for recording information. Always reconcile your checkbook with your monthly bank statement and record any service charges, check purchases, and interest earned. Your checkbook information will be transferred to your Revenue & Expense Journal where you do your bookkeeping.

♦ *Customer Records (or Databases).* These records are kept as a means of helping a business deal more effectively with its customers. The

Payable: ready to be paid. One of the standard accounts kept by a bookkeeper is "accounts payable." This is a list of those bills that are current and due to be paid.

Receivable: ready for payment. When you sell on credit, you keep an "accounts receivable" ledger as a record of what is owed to you and who owes it. In accounting, a receivable is an asset.

Bank statement: a monthly statement of account which a bank renders to each of its depositors.

TECH TIP 17
Database Software

It is a common practice to set up database files using software such as Microsoft Access, Q&A, Paradox, or any of a variety offered today. The software will allow you to customize fields of information that can be accessed at the click of a mouse, generating targeted mailing lists, sales information, demographics, etc. You can also print mailing labels and customized letters. With the search functions, you can narrow any list down to only those customers who meet the requirements of your current focus. It is important again to remember as you set-up your database files and customize your fields, that the output will only be as good as the input.

type you keep is purely subjective. The basic idea is that you keep the information that will enable you to sell more of your products or services to the customer, give the customer better service, and have the information you need regarding your transactions with them at your disposal. The database can be as simple or as complicated as you choose. A simple example of hand-generated customer files might be a set of 3 x 5 cards, one for each customer, with specialized information such as name, address, telephone number, services rendered, products sold, and any other information that will help you to better serve the customer. Customer records are especially effective in service industries or in small businesses dealing in specialty retail sales.

Financial Statements

Financial statements are developed from the general records discussed on the preceding pages. These statements are used to provide information for preparing tax returns. Even more importantly, the use of these financial statements can help you see the financial condition of your business and identify its relative strengths and weaknesses. The business owner who takes the time to understand and evaluate his or her operation through financial statements will be far ahead of the entrepreneur who is concerned only with the product or service.

We will now introduce you to the two principal financial statements of any business: the Balance Sheet and the Profit & Loss Statement.

Balance sheet. The balance sheet is a financial statement that shows the condition of your business as of a fixed date. It is most effectively done at the end of every accounting period. *(If you are using accounting software, a balance sheet can be easily generated at the close of the*

> **Accounting period:** a time interval at the end of which an analysis is made of the information contained in the bookkeeping records. Also the period of time covered by the profit & loss statement.

accounting period.) The closing balances from your general records will supply you with the information.

The balance sheet can be likened to a still photograph. It is the picture of your firm's financial condition at a given moment and will show whether your financial position is strong or weak. Examination of this statement will allow you to analyze your business and implement timely modifications.

A balance sheet lists a business's assets, liabilities, and net worth (or capital). The assets are everything your business owns that has monetary value (cash, inventory, fixed assets, etc.). Liabilities are the debts owed by the business to any of its creditors. The net worth (or owner's equity) represents the cumulative profits and losses of the company plus or minus any equity deposits or withdrawals. The relationship between assets, liabilities, and net worth can be seen in the following well-known accounting formula:

Assets – Liabilities = Net worth

If a business possesses more assets than it owes to its creditors (liabilities), then its net worth will be positive. If the business owes more than it possesses, its net worth will be a negative. (See filled-in example on page 158.)

Current liabilities: Amounts owed that will ordinarily be paid by a company within one year. Generally includes accounts payable, current portion of long-term debt, interest, and dividends payable.

Profit & loss statement (income statement). This financial statement shows your business' financial activity over a specific period of time. Unlike the balance sheet, a profit & loss statement can be likened to a moving picture. It shows where your money came from and where it was spent over a specific period of time. You will be able to pick out weaknesses in your operation and plan ways to run your business more effectively, thereby increasing your profits.

A profit & loss statement should be prepared at the close of each month. The totals from your revenue & expense journal are transferred to the corresponding columns of the profit & loss statement. At the end of December (or your tax year) you will have a clear picture of your revenues and expenses for the 12-month period. *(Accounting software is also set up to generate both monthly and annual profit & loss statements for your business.)*

Comparison of the profit & loss statements from several years will reveal such trends in your business as high revenue periods, effective advertising times, increases or decreases in profit margins, and a host of other valuable information. Do not underestimate the value of this important tool.

Just as the balance sheet has an accepted format, a profit & loss sheet must contain certain categories in a particular order. A filled-in example of this financial statement can be found at the end of the chapter on page 159.

General Recordkeeping Schedule

There is a specific order to recordkeeping. It must be done in a timely manner if the records are to be effective. Since the two goals of record-keeping are the retrieval of tax information and the analysis of information for internal planning, your schedule will have to provide for these goals. The tasks are listed according to frequency: daily, weekly, monthly, and end of the year. Schedules for filing tax information are not included. They can be found in IRS Publication #334, *Tax Guide for Small Business*.

Free IRS Publications

The Internal Revenue Service provides many free publications that will be helpful to you as a small business owner. Information on ordering all publications may be obtained by calling the IRS toll free at 1-800-TAX-FORM (1-800-829-3276). It is a good idea to start your tax publication file by asking for Publication #334, *Tax Guide for Small Business*. This publication provides a comprehensive overview on most tax topics. Other publications deal in more specific information relating to individual topics such as: Business Use of Your Car, Legal Structure, Depreciation, etc. If you subscribe to an online service, the IRS offers the ability to download electronic print files of current tax forms, instructions, and taxpayer information publications. IRS at FedWorld can be reached at their Web site: www.ustreas.gov.

 Note: The **General Recordkeeping Schedule**, located on the next page, will help you to organize your bookkeeping chores. We suggest you make a copy of it and keep it with your records. It should serve as a basic guide for the person who has no recordkeeping experience.

 TECH TIP 18

Access IRS Information by Computer and Modem

The IRS offers the ability to download and print out electronic print files of current tax forms, instructions, and taxpayer information publications (TIPs) in three different file formats. Internal Revenue Information Services (IRS) is housed within FedWorld, known also as the Electronic Marketplace of U.S. government information, a broadly accessible electronic bulletin board system. FedWorld offers direct dial-up access, as well as Internet connectivity, and provides "gateway" access to more than 140 different government bulletin boards.

IRIS at FedWorld can be reached by:

1. Modem (dial-up) the Internal Revenue Information Services bulletin board at 703-321-8020

2. Telnet—iris.irs.ustreas.gov

3. File Transfer Protocol (FTP)—connect to ftp.irs.ustreas.gov, or

4. World Wide Web—www.ustreas.gov

General Recordkeeping Schedule

(Post for your convenience)

Daily

- Go through mail and sort according to action needed.

- Unpack and shelve incoming inventory.

- Record inventory information.

- Pay any invoices necessary to meet discount deadlines.

Weekly

- Prepare income deposit.

- Enter deposit in checkbook and Revenue & Expense Journal.

- Enter sales information in Inventory Record.

- Enter week's checking transactions in Revenue & Expense Journal.

- Record petty cash purchases in Petty Cash Record. File receipts.

- Pay invoices due. Be aware of discount dates. File invoices.

- Enter other purchases (such as fixed assets) in appropriate records.

Monthly

- Balance checkbook and reconcile with bank statement.

- Enter interest earned and bank charges in Revenue & Expense Journal and checkbook.

- Total and balance all Revenue & Expense Journal columns.

- Check Accounts Receivable and send out statements.

- Prepare monthly Profit & Loss Statement and Balance Sheet.

End of the Year

- Pay all invoices, sales taxes, and other expenses you wish to use as deductions for the current year.

- Transfer 12th month totals from the Revenue & Expense Journal to the Profit & Loss Statement.

- Total the horizontal columns of the Profit & Loss Statement to get yearly totals for each category.

- Prepare an end-of-the-year Balance Sheet.

- Using your 12-month Profit & Loss Statement, prepare a Cash Flow Statement for the coming year.

- Set-up new records for the coming year.

Ace Sporting Goods
Revenue & Expense Journal

July 2000, page 2

CHECK NO.	DATE	TRANSACTION	REVENUE	EXPENSE	SALES	SALES TAX	SERV-ICES	INV. PURCH	ADVERT	FREIGHT	OFF SUPP	MISC
		Balance forward----	1,826 00	835 00	1,218 00	98 00	510 00	295 00	245 00	150 00	83 50	61 50
234	7/13	J. J. Advertising		450 00					450 00			
235	7/13	T & E Products		380 00				380 00				
236	7/16	Regal Stationers		92 50							92 50	
***	7/17	Deposit:	1,232 00									
		1. Sales (taxable)			400 00	32 00						
		2. Sales (out of state)			165 00	O.S.						
		3. Sales (resale)			370 00	Resale						
		4. Services					265 00					
O.K. BANK	7/19	Bank charges		23 40								(bank chg) 23 40
237	7/19	Petty Cash deposit		100 00								(p/cash) 100 00
		TOTALS	3,058 00	1,880 90	2,153 00	130 00	775 00	675 00	695 00	150 00	176 00	184 90

Ace Sporting Goods
Petty Cash Record

PETTY CASH - 2000					Page 6
DATE	**PAID TO WHOM**	**EXPENSE ACCOUNT DEBITED**	**DEPOSIT**	**AMOUNT OF EXPENSE**	**BALANCE**
	BALANCE FORWARD ⎯⎯⎯⎯⎯				10 00
Jul. 19	✳✳ Deposit (Ck. 237)		100 00		110 00
20	ACE Hardware	Maintenance		12 36	97 64
23	Regal Stationers	Office Supplies		20 00	77 64
23	U.S. Postmaster	Postage		19 80	57 84
31	The Steak House	Meals		63 75	(5 91)
Aug 1	✳✳ Deposit (Ck.267)		100 00		94 09

Toward the end of the year, you can let the Petty Cash account run a minus balance. On December 31st, a check is written for the balance and the account is zeroed out.

The amount of cash spent during the year will be exactly equal to the amount deposited into the Petty Cash Account from your checking account.

NOTE:
1. Save all receipts for cash purchases.
2. Exchange receipt for cash from petty cash drawer.
3. Use receipts to record expenses on petty cash form.
4. File receipts. You may need them for verification.
5. Be sure to record petty cash deposits.

Ace Sporting Goods Inventory Record
Non-Identifiable Stock

DEPARTMENT/CATEGORY: *Ski Hats / Headwear*

PRODUCTION OR PURCHASE DATE	INVENTORY PURCHASED OR MANUFACTURED		NUMBER OF UNITS	UNIT COST		VALUE ON DATE OF INVENTORY (Unit Cost X Units on Hand)	
	Stock #	Description				Value	Date
2/05/98	07-43	Knitted Headbands	5,000	2	50	0	1/00
3/25/98	19-12	Face Masks	3,000	5	12	450.80	1/00
9/14/98	19-10	Hat/Mask Combo	1,200	7	00	3,514.00	1/00
4/18/99	19-09	Hats, Multi-Colored	10,500	4	00	5,440.00	1/00
8/31/99	19-07	Gortex (w/bill)	10,000	8	41	50,460.00	1/00
BEGIN 2000							
2/01/00	19-12	Face Masks	2,500	4	80		
2/28/00	19-09	Hats, Multi-Colored	10,300	4	00		

NOTE: 1. This record is used for inventory of like items that are purchased or manufactured in bulk. It is a good idea to divide your records by department, category, or by manufacturer.

2. Inventory these items by a physical count or by computer records. A physical inventory is required at the close of your tax year.

3. Inventory is valued according to rules that apply for **FIFO** or **LIFO.** Read the information in your tax guide carefully before determining inventory value. The selected method must be used consistently.

Ace Sporting Goods Inventory Record
Identifiable Stock

WHOLESALER: *Anderson Custom Designs*					Page _1_

PURCH. DATE	INVENTORY PURCHASED		PURCH. PRICE	DATE SOLD	SALE PRICE	NAME OF BUYER (Optional)
	Stock #	Description				
1/16/00	Blue M	Golf Design	16 00	2/24/00	32 00	J. Pearce
1/23/00	Red S	Tennis T-Shirts	12 00			
	Red M	Baseball T-Shirt	12 00			
	Blue L	Soccer T-Shirt	12 00	2/07/00	24 00	S. Wong
2/16/00	Wt. L	Golf T-Shirt	14 00	3/01/00	26 00	K. Lee
3/16/00	Wt. M	Soccer T-Shirt	14 00			
3/16/00	Gr. L	Tennis T-Shirt	14 00			
	Gr. M	Basketball T-Shirt	14 00			

NOTE: 1. Use this record for keeping track of identifiable goods purchased for resale. If your inventory is very large, it may be necessary to use some sort of **Point-of-Sale** inventory system.

2. Each page should deal with either: (1) purchases in one category, or (2) goods purchased from one wholesaler.

3. Use the name of the wholesaler or the category of the purchase as the heading.

Ace Sporting Goods
Fixed Assets Log

COMPANY NAME: _Ace Sporting Goods_

ASSET PURCHASED	DATE PLACED IN SERVICE	COST OF ASSET	% USED FOR BUSINESS	RECOVERY PERIOD	METHOD OF DEPRECIATION	DEPRECIATION PREVIOUSLY ALLOWED	DATE SOLD	SALE PRICE
1994 Dodge Van	1/08/95	18,700 00	80%	5 yr.	200% DB	15,469 00	9/12/99	8,500 00
IBM Computer	7/15/96	6,450 00	100%	5 yr.	200% DB	3,620 00		
Ricoh Copier	12/29/96	3,000 00	100%	5 yr.	S/L-DB	1,469 00		
Climbing Simulator	6/17/99	4,500 00	100%	15 yr.	150% DB	—		
1999 Dodge Van	8/05/99	21,000 00	80%	5 yr.	200% DB	—		
Tennis ProString	3/15/00	1,500 00	100%	7 yr.	200% DB	—		

NOTE: See IRS Publication 334, *Tax Guide for Small Business*, for more detailed information on depreciation. Also see Publications 534, 544, and 551.

Ace Sporting Goods
Accounts Payable
Account Record

CREDITOR:: _Johnson Mills_

ADDRESS: _7222 Main Street_
Johnson, NV 26401

TEL. NO: _(800) 555-7201_   ACCOUNT NO. _2012_

INVOICE DATE	INVOICE NO.	INVOICE AMOUNT		TERMS	DATE PAID	AMOUNT PAID		INVOICE BALANCE	
2/16/00	264	600	00	Net 30	3/07/00	600	00	0	00
3/16/00	326	300	00	Net 30	4/15/00	300	00	0	00
6/20/00	417	1,200	00	N30/2%10	6/26/00	1,176	00	0	00
8/26/00	816	2,000	00	N30/2%10	9/01/00	500	00	1,500	00

Ace Sporting Goods
Accounts Receivable
Account Record

CUSTOMER: _Martin's Team Shoppe_

ADDRESS: _222 Stevens Road_
Winnemucca, NV 89502

TEL. NO: _(702) 864-2222_   ACCOUNT NO. _1024_

INVOICE DATE	INVOICE NO.	INVOICE AMOUNT		TERMS	DATE PAID	AMOUNT PAID		INVOICE BALANCE	
3/16/00	3621	240	00	Net 30	4/12/00	240	00	0	00
4/19/00	5400	316	00	Net 30	4/30/00	316	00	0	00
5/20/00	6172	525	00	N30/2%10	5/26/00	514	50	0	00
6/16/00	7511	800	00	N30/2%10	7/14/00	250	00	550	00
7/12/00	7633	386	00	N30/2%10				386	00

Ace Sporting Goods
Mileage Log

NAME: _Ace Sporting Goods (John Kelley)_

DATED: From _July 1_ **To** _July 31, 2000_

DATE	CITY OF DESTINATION	NAME OR OTHER DESIGNATION	BUSINESS PURPOSE	NO. OF MILES
7-01	San Diego, CA	Convention Center	California Sports Expo	187 mi.
7-03	Cypress, CA	The Print Co.	p/u brochures	13 mi.
7-04	Long Beach, CA	Wm. Long High	Deliver Uniforms	53 mi.
7-07	Fullerton, CA	Bank of America	Loan Meeting	17 mi.
7-17	Los Angees, CA	Moore Corp.	Negotiate inventory purchase	96 mi.
7-23	Los Angeles, CA	IDT	Consultation	113 mi.
			TOTAL MILES THIS SHEET	479

NOTE: 1. A mileage record is required by the IRS to claim a mileage deduction. It is also used to determine the percentage of business use of a car.

2. Keep your mileage log in your vehicle and record your mileage as it occurs. It is very difficult to recall after the fact.

Ace Sporting Goods
Entertainment Expense Record

NAME: _John Kelley_

DATED: From _7-01-00_ To _7-31-00_

DATE	PLACE OF ENTERTAINMENT	BUSINESS PURPOSE	NAME OF PERSON ENTERTAINED	AMOUNT SPENT	
7-01	The 410 Club	Sell Uniform Line	William Long	46	32
7-07	Seafood Chef	Consult w/attorney	Thomas Moore	23	50
7 -18	The Cannon Club	Staff Dinner	Company Employees	384	00

NOTE: For more information on Meals and Entertainment, please refer to IRS Publication 463, *Travel, Entertainment and Gift Expenses*.

Ace Sporting Goods Travel Record

TRIP TO: _Dallas, Texas_

Dated From: _7-11-00_ To: _7-16-00_

Business Purpose: _Sports Technology Expo (show exhibitor)_

No. Days Spent on Business _6_

DATE	LOCATION	EXPENSE PAID TO	MEALS				HOTEL	TAXIS, ETC.	AUTOMOBILE			MISC EXP
			Breakfast	Lunch	Dinner	Misc.			Gas	Parking	Tolls	
7-11	Phoenix, AZ	Mobil Gas				6 40			21 00			
7-11	Phoenix, AZ	Greentree Inn		12 50								
7-11	Chola, NM	Exxon							23 50			
7-11	Las Cruces, NM	Holiday Inn			27 00		49 00					
7-12	Las Cruces, NM	Exxon							19 00			
7-12	Taft, TX	Molly's Cafe		16 25								
7-12	Dallas, TX	Holiday Inn			18 75		54 00					
7-13	Dallas, TX	Expo Center								8 00		
7-13	Dallas, TX	Harvey's Eatery		21 00								
7-13	Dallas, TX	Holiday Inn			24 50		54 00					
7-14	Dallas, TX	Holiday Inn	9 50									(Fax) 9 00
7-14	Dallas, TX	Expo Center		14 00						8 00		
7-14	Dallas, TX	Holiday Inn			16 20		54 00					
7-15	Pokie, TX	Texaco							21 00			
7-15	Pokie, TX	Denny's		18 50								
7-15	Chola, NM	Holiday Inn			27 00		48 00					
7-16	Chola, NM	Holiday Inn	12 75									
7-16	Flagstaff, AZ	Texaco							22 00			
TOTALS →			22 25	83 25	113 45	6 40	259 00		106 50	16 00		9 00

Attach all receipts for Meals, Hotel, Fares, Auto, Entertainment, etc. Details of your expenses can be noted on the receipts. File your travel record and your receipts in the same envelope. Label the envelope as to trip made. File all travel records together. When expenses are allocated, be sure not to double expense anything. (Ex: Gas cannot be used if you elect to use mileage as the basis for deducting your car expenses.)

Balance Sheet

Business Name: **Ace Sporting Goods**   **Date: September 30, 2000**

ASSETS

Current assets

Cash	$	8,742
Petty cash	$	167
Accounts receivable	$	5,400
Inventory	$	101,800
Short-term investments	$	0
Prepaid expenses	$	1,967

Long-term investments $ 0

Fixed assets

Land (valued at cost)		$	185,000
Buildings		$	143,000
1. Cost	171,600		
2. Less acc. depr.	28,600		
Improvements		$	0
1. Cost			
2. Less acc. depr.			
Equipment		$	5,760
1. Cost	7,200		
2. Less acc. depr.	1,440		
Furniture		$	2,150
1. Cost	2,150		
2. Less acc. depr.	0		
Autos/vehicles		$	16,432
1. Cost	19,700		
2. Less acc. depr.	3,268		

Other assets

1.	$	
2.	$	

TOTAL ASSETS $ 470,418

LIABILITIES

Current liabilities

Accounts payable	$	2,893
Notes payable	$	0
Interest payable	$	1,842
Taxes payable		
Federal income tax	$	5,200
Self-employment tax	$	1,025
State income tax	$	800
Sales tax accrual	$	2,130
Property tax	$	0
Payroll accrual	$	4,700

Long-term liabilities

Notes payable	$	196,700

TOTAL LIABILITIES $ 215,290

NET WORTH (EQUITY)

Proprietorship	$	
or		
Partnership		
John Smith, 60% equity	$	153,077
Mary Blake, 40% equity	$	102,051
or		
Corporation		
Capital stock	$	
Surplus paid in	$	
Retained earnings	$	

TOTAL NET WORTH $ 255,128

Assets – Liabilities = Net Worth
and
Liabilities + Equity = Total Assets

Profit & Loss (Income) Statement
Ace Sporting Goods

Beginning: January 1, 2000   **Ending: December 31, 2000**

INCOME		
1. Sales revenues		$ 500,000
2. Cost of goods sold (c – d)		312,000
a. Beginning inventory (1/01)	147,000	
b. Purchases	320,000	
c. C.O.G. avail. sale (a + b)	467,000	
d. Less ending inventory (12/31)	155,000	
3. Gross profit on sales (1 – 2)		$ 188,000
EXPENSES		
1. Variable (selling) (a thru h)		67,390
a. Advertising/marketing	14,000	
b. Freight	9,000	
c. Fulfillment of orders	2,000	
d. Packaging costs	33,000	
e. Salaries/wages/commissions	3,000	
f. Travel	1,650	
g. Misc. variable (selling) expense	390	
h. Depreciation (prod/serv assets)	4,350	
2. Fixed (administrative) (a thru h)		51,610
a. Financial administration	1,000	
b. Insurance	3,800	
c. Licenses and permits	2,710	
d. Office salaries	14,000	
e. Rent expense	22,500	
f. Utilities	3,000	
g. Misc. fixed (administrative) expense	0	
h. Depreciation (office equipment)	4,600	
Total operating expenses (1 + 2)		119,000
Net Income from operations (GP – Exp)		$ 69,000
Other income (interest income)		5,000
Other expense (interest expense)		7,000
Net profit (loss) before taxes		$ 67,000
Taxes		
a. Federal	21,000	
b. State	4,500	26,000
c. Local	500	
NET PROFIT (LOSS) AFTER TAXES		$ 41,000

Success or Failure: It Depends on Your Cash Flow

I t is a fact that a third or more of today's businesses fail due to a lack of cash flow. What is cash flow? How do you plan ahead to ensure your chances of success? The purpose of this chapter will be to introduce you to the concept of "cash flow" and to show you how careful planning can help you avoid business disaster.

❖ ❖ ❖ ❖ ❖

What Is a Cash Flow Statement?

The Pro Forma Cash Flow Statement is the financial document that **projects** what your business plan means in terms of dollars. A cash flow statement is the same as a budget. It is a pro forma (or projected) statement used for internal planning and estimates how much money will flow into and out of a business during a designated period of time, usually the coming tax year. Your profit at the end of the year will depend on the proper balance between cash inflow and outflow.

The **Cash Flow Statement** identifies when cash is expected to be received and when it must be spent to pay bills and debts. It also allows the manager to identify where the necessary cash will come from.

This statement deals only with **actual cash transactions** and not with depreciation and amortization of goodwill or other noncash expense items. Expenses are paid from cash on hand, sale of assets, revenues from sales and services, interest earned on investments, money borrowed from a lender, and influx of capital in exchange for equity in

Cash flow: the actual movement of cash within a business; the analysis of how much cash is needed and when that money is required by a business within a period of time.

Pro forma: a projection or estimate of what may result in the future from actions in the present; shows how the actual operations of the business will turn out if certain assumptions are achieved.

Administrative expense: expenses chargeable to the managerial, general, administrative and policy phases of a business in contrast to sales, manufacturing, or cost of goods expense.

the company. If your business will require $100,000 to pay its expenses and $50,000 to support the owners, you will need at least an equal amount of money flowing into the business just to maintain the status quo. Anything less will eventually lead to an inability to pay your creditors or yourself.

Webster's New World Dictionary defines cash flow as "the pattern of receipts and expenditures of a company, government, etc., resulting in the availability or nonavailability of cash." The availability or nonavailability of cash when it is needed for expenditures gets to the very heart of the matter. By careful planning, you must try to project not only **how much** cash will have to flow into and out of your business, but also **when** it will need to flow in and out. A business may be able to plan for gross receipts that will cover its needs. However, if those sales do not take place in time to pay the expenses, your venture will soon be history unless you plan ahead for other sources of cash to tide the business over until the revenues are realized. The publishing industry is a good example of a business that has heavy cash demands as many as six to nine months before it realizes any revenues as a result of those expenditures. If a publisher cannot pay the printer, there will be no books for sale. The printer will not produce the finished product on a promise that he or she will be paid nine months later at the completion of sales and receipt of invoice payments. To keep the business going, the publisher must plan ahead for sources of cash to tide the business over until the revenues are received.

Preplanning Worksheets

Because the cash flow statement deals with cash inflow and cash outflow, the first step in planning can be best accomplished by preparing two worksheets.

1. *Cash to Be Paid Out.* Cash flowing out of your business. See pages 164–165. This worksheet documents the cash flowing out of your business. It identifies categories of expenses and obligations and the projected amount of cash needed in each category. You may wish to approach this task by compiling several individual budgets (inventory purchases, direct expenses, administrative expenses, owner draws, etc.)

These expenditures are not always easy to estimate. If yours is a new business, it will be necessary for you to do lots of market research. If you are an existing business, you will combine information from past financial statements with trends in your particular industry.

2. ***Sources of Cash.*** Cash flowing into your business. See the worksheet on pages 166–167. Use this worksheet to document the cash flowing into your business. It will help you to estimate how much cash will be available and from what sources. To complete this worksheet, you will have to look at cash on hand, projected revenues, assets that can be liquidated, possible lenders or investors and owner equity to be contributed. This worksheet will force you to take a look at any existing possibilities for increasing available cash.

Marketing research: the systematic design, collection, analysis, and reporting of data regarding a specific marketing situation.

On the next four pages, you will see examples of the two worksheets along with accompanying information explaining each of the categories used. The worksheets are filled in for our fictitious company, **Ace Sporting Goods**, to help you understand the process. **Please note** that the Cash to Be Paid Out Worksheet shows a need for $131,000. It was necessary in projecting Sources of Cash to account for $131,000 without the projected sales because payment is not expected to be received until November and December (too late for cash needs in January through October). Next year, those revenues will be reflected in cash on hand or other salable assets.

When you do your own worksheets:

◈ Try to be as realistic as possible. **Do not overstate revenues and/or understate expenses**, a deadly error frequently made during the planning process.

◈ Be sure to figure all of your estimates on both worksheets for the same time period (i.e., annually, quarterly, or monthly).

Cash to Be Paid Out Worksheet

Explanation of Categories

1. **Start-up costs**

   These are the costs incurred by you to get your business underway. They are generally one-time expenses and are capitalized for tax purposes.

2. **Inventory purchases**

   Cash to be spent during the period on items intended for resale. If you purchase manufactured products, this includes the cash outlay for those purchases. If you are the manufacturer, include labor and materials on units to be produced.

3. **Variable expenses (selling or direct expenses)**

   These are the costs of all expenses that will relate directly to your product or service (other than manufacturing costs or purchase price of inventory).

4. **Fixed expenses (administrative or indirect expenses)**

   Include all expected costs of office overhead. If certain bills must be paid ahead, include total cash outlay even if covered period extends into the next year.

5. **Assets (long-term purchases)**

   These are the capital assets that will be depreciated over a period of years (land, buildings, vehicles, equipment). Determine how you intend to pay for them and include all cash to be paid out in the current period. Note: Land is the only asset that does not depreciate and will be listed at cost.

6. **Liabilities**

   What are the payments you expect to have to make to retire any debts or loans? Do you have any Accounts Payable as you begin the new year? You will need to determine the amount of cash outlay that needs to be paid in the current year. If you have a car loan for $20,000 and you pay $500 per month for 12 months, you will have a cash outlay of $6,000 for the coming year.

7. **Owner equity**

   This item is frequently overlooked in planning cash flow. If you, as the business owner, will need a draw of $2,000 per month to live on, you must plan for $24,000 cash flowing out of your business. Failure to plan for it will result in a cash flow shortage and may cause your business to fail.

Note: Be sure to use the same time period throughout your worksheet.

* Variable & Fixed Expense Categories Must Be Determined By You *

Every business has expenses that are specific to its industry. You will have to customize your variable and fixed expense categories to match your business. We have suggested some in our examples to get you started. You will type in your own headings in the working spreadsheets. As you begin to operate your business, you will be better able to determine what your true expenditures are. You can change later if you find that your current categories do not meet your needs.

Cash to Be Paid Out Worksheet
(Cash Flowing Out of the Business)

Business Name: Ace Sporting Goods   Time Period Covered: Jan 1–Dec 31, 2000

1. START-UP COSTS		1,450
Business license	30	
Corporation filing	500	
Legal fees	920	
Other start-up costs:		
a.		
b.		
c.		
d.		
2. INVENTORY PURCHASES		
Cash out for goods intended for resale		32,000
3. VARIABLE EXPENSES (SELLING)		
Advertising/marketing	6,000	
Event planning	2,500	
Freight	800	
Packaging costs	14,000	
Sales salaries/commissions	2,000	
Travel	1,550	
Miscellaneous	300	
TOTAL SELLING EXPENSES		27,150
4. FIXED EXPENSES (ADMINISTRATION)		
Financial administration	1,800	
Insurance	900	
Licenses and permits	100	
Office salaries	16,300	
Rent expense	8,600	
Utilities	2,400	
Miscellaneous	400	
TOTAL ADMINISTRATIVE EXPENSE		30,500
5. ASSETS (LONG-TERM PURCHASES)		6,000
Cash to be paid out in current period		
6. LIABILITIES		9,900
Cash outlay for retiring debts, loans, and/or accounts payable		
7. OWNER EQUITY		
Cash to be withdrawn by owner		24,000
TOTAL CASH TO BE PAID OUT		**$131,000**

Sources of Cash Worksheet

Explanation of Categories

1. **Cash on hand**

Money that you have on hand. Be sure to include petty cash and moneys not yet deposited.

2. **Sales (revenues)**

This includes projected revenues from the sale of your product and/or service. If payment is not expected during the time period covered by this worksheet, do not include that portion of your sales. Think about the projected timing of sales. If receipts will be delayed beyond the time when a large amount of cash is needed, make a notation to that effect and take it into consideration when determining the need for temporary financing. Include deposits you require on expected sales or services. To figure collections on accounts receivable, you will have to project the percentage of invoices that will be lost to bad debts and subtract it from your accounts receivable total.

3. **Miscellaneous income**

Do you, or will you have, any moneys out on loan or deposited in accounts that will yield interest income during the period in question?

4. **Sale of long-term assets**

If you are expecting to sell any of your fixed assets such as land, buildings, vehicles, machinery, equipment, etc., be sure to include only the cash you will receive during the current period.

Important: At this point in your worksheet, add up all sources of cash. If you do not have an amount equal to your projected needs, you will have to plan sources of cash covered under numbers 5 and 6.

5. **Liabilities**

This figure represents the amount you will be able to borrow from lending institutions such as banks, finance companies, the SBA, etc. Be reasonable about what you think you can borrow. If you have no collateral, have no business plan, or if you have a poor financial history, you will find it difficult, if not impossible, to find a lender. This source of cash requires preplanning.

6. **Equity**

Sources of equity come from owner investments, contributed capital, sale of stock, or venture capital. Do you anticipate the availability of personal funds? Does your business have the potential for growth that might interest a venture capitalist? Be sure to be realistic in this area. You cannot sell stock (or equity) to a nonexistent investor.

Sources of Cash Worksheet

(Cash Flowing Into the Business)

Business Name: Ace Sporting Goods

Time Period Covered: From January 1, 2000 to December 31, 2000

1. CASH ON HAND	$20,000
2. SALES (REVENUES)	
Product sales income*	90,000
Most of this sales revenue will not be received until Nov. or Dec.	
Services income	22,000
Deposits on sales or services	0
Collections on accounts receivable	3,000
3. MISCELLANEOUS INCOME	
Interest income	1,000
Payments to be received on loans	0
4. SALE OF LONG-TERM ASSETS	0
5. LIABILITIES	40,000
Loan funds (to be received during current period, from banks, through the SBA, or from other lending institutions)	
6. EQUITY	
Owner investments (sole proprietors/partners)	10,000
Contributed capital (corporation)	
Sale of stock (corporation)	
Venture capital	35,000
A. Without product sales =	**$131,000**
TOTAL CASH AVAILABLE	
B. With product sales =	**$221,000**

Using the Worksheets to Build the Cash Flow Statement

Now that you have completed the two worksheets, you are ready to use that information. You have estimated how much cash will be needed for the year and you now know what sources are available. In the next phase of cash flow planning you will break the time period of one year into monthly segments and predict when the cash will be needed to make the financial year flow smoothly. To make the job easier, you can follow these steps:

◆ Figure the cost of goods and the variable and fixed expenses in monthly increments. Most will vary. When do you plan to purchase the most inventory? What months will require the most advertising? Are you expecting a rent or insurance premium increase? When will commissions be due on expected sales?

◆ Project sales on a monthly basis based on payment of invoices, demand for your particular product or service, and on how readily you can fill that demand. There will be no cash flowing in for orders that have not been filled and invoices that are not paid. If you are in a service business and you have no employees other than yourself, remember that income ceases when you are on vacation.

◆ Determine your depreciable asset needs. When will you need them? How much will the payments be and when will they begin?

◆ Fill in as much of the cash flow statement as you can using these projections and any others that you can comfortably determine. Then proceed according to the directions and complete the rest.

How to Fill In the Forms

To clarify the process of filling in a cash flow statement, pages 170 and 171 have been devoted to walking you through January and part of February for Ace Sporting Goods.

Pages 172 and 173 contain the directions for completing a **Pro Forma Cash Flow Statement** and a sample statement. There is also a blank form located in Appendix B for you to use to make your own projection.

Remember

The **Pro Forma Cash Flow Statement** is one of the most useful financial tools available to the small business owner. It is also the first financial projection to be examined by a lender or investor because it shows how you plan to make it through the year, repaying your loan plus interest and at the same time maintaining the necessary cash flow to operate the business for maximum profitability.

TECH TIP 19

Save Your Valuable Time: Use Preformatted and Preformulated Spreadsheets

Planning your cash flow takes time in two ways: First you will have to spend the time to research all of your information and form your organizational and marketing concepts. Once you have your ideas, you will then have to interpret everything you want to do into numbers so that you will be able to analyze the projected results.

Building your cash flow statement (budget) is a long and tedious process, especially if you are trying to do it with a pencil and a piece of paper. There are about 350+ numbers to fill in and calculate. The job becomes compounded if you make a change and have to recalculate your numbers.

Computer Spreadsheets Will Solve Your Problems

Software programs such as Excel® and Lotus® enable the user to build and formulate spreadsheets that will automatically perform complex calculations in an instant. Every computer user should learn to use one of these programs.

Even more pertinent, in this instance, is the ability to access spreadsheets (such as in our business planning software) that have already been developed specifically for use in making cash flow projections. These spreadsheets are already preformatted as Cash Flow Statements and they are preformulated to instantly perform the calculations any time you input a number. **Caution:** Be sure you can customize the form to your own chart of accounts.

What-If Scenarios

The best part about using preformatted and preformulated computer spreadsheets is that you can try out different scenarios for your business, (add a product or service, buy a piece of equipment, or cut back on an expense). Input the new numbers and you will instantly be able to see what the probable financial effect will be on your business.

Ace Sporting Goods

Cash Flow for January and February 2000

January Projections

1. Ace Sporting Goods projects a beginning cash balance of $20,000.
2. Cash Receipts: The store has not opened, so there will be no sales. However, income of $4,000 is projected on receivables from a previous location.
3. Interest on the $20,000 will amount to about $50 at current rate.
4. There are no long-term assets to sell. Enter a zero.
5. Adding 1, 2, 3, and 4 the Total Cash Available will be $23,050.
6. Cash Payments: Inventory payment will not be due until February. However, there will be graphic design costs of $5,000 for local team uniforms.
7. Variable (Selling) Expenses: Estimated at $1,140.
8. Fixed (Administrative): Estimated at $1,215.
9. Interest Expense: No outstanding debts or loans. Enter zero.
10. Taxes: No profit for previous quarter. No estimated taxes would be due.
11. Payments on Long-Term Assets: Ace Sporting Goods plans to purchase office equipment to be paid in full at the time of purchase. Enter $1,139.
12. Loan Repayments: No loans have been received. Enter zero.
13. Owner Draws: Owner will need $2,000 for living expenses.
14. Total Cash Paid Out: Add 6 through 13. Total $10,494
15. Cash Balance: Subtract Cash Paid Out from Total Cash Available. Enter $13,556.
16. Loans to be Received: Being aware of the $30,000 inventory costs payable in February, a loan of $40,000 is anticipated to increase Cash Available. (This requires advance planning!)
17. Equity Deposit: Owner plans to add $5,000 from personal account.
18. Ending Cash Balance: Adding 15, 16, and 17 the sum is $58,556.

February Projections

1. Beginning Cash Balance: January's Ending Cash Balance is transferred to February's Beginning Balance. Enter $58,556.
2. Cash Receipts: Coaching clinic income of $1,000 plus $1,000 to be collected from opening sales at the end of the month. $2,000.
3. Interest Income: Projected at about $60.
4. Sale of Long-Term Assets: None. Enter zero.
5. Total Cash Available: Add 1, 2, 3, and 4. The result is $60,616.
6. Cash Payments: $30,000 due for store inventory. $400 due for graphic design.
7. Continue as in January. Don't forget to include payments on the loan that was received in January.

Ace Sporting Goods
Partial Cash Flow Statement

	Jan	Feb
BEGINNING CASH BALANCE	20,000	58,556
CASH RECEIPTS		
A. Sales/revenues	4,000	2,000
B. Receivables	0	0
C. Interest income	50	60
D. Sale of long-term assets	0	0
TOTAL CASH AVAILABLE	23,050	60,616
CASH PAYMENTS		
A. Cost of goods to be sold		
1. Purchases	0	30,000
2. Material	0	0
3. Labor	5,000	400
Total Cost of Goods	5,000	30,400
B. Variable Expenses (Selling)		
1. Advertising/marketing	470	
2. Event planning	320	
3. Freight	0	
4. Sales salaries/commissions	0	
5. Travel	0	
6. Vehicle	285	
7. Miscellaneous selling expense	165	
Total Variable Expenses	1,140	
C. Fixed Expenses (Administrative)		
1. Financial administration	80	
2. Insurance	125	
3. License/permits	200	
4. Office salaries	500	
5. Rent expenses	110	
6. Utilities	200	
7. Miscellaneous administrative expense	0	
Total Fixed Expenses	1,215	
D. Interest expense	0	
E. Federal income tax	0	
F. Other uses	0	
G. Long-term asset payments	1,139	
H. Loan payments	0	
I. Owner draws	2,000	
TOTAL CASH PAID OUT	10,494	
CASH BALANCE/DEFICIENCY	13,556	
Loans to be received	40,000	
Equity deposits	5,000	
ENDING CASH BALANCE	58,556	

CONTINUE as in JANUARY

Directions for Completing a Cash Flow Statement

This page contains instructions for completing the cash flow statement on the next page. A blank form for your own projections can be found in Appendix B.

Vertical Columns are divided into twelve months and preceded by a "Total Column."

Horizontal Positions on the statement contain all sources of cash and cash to be paid out. The figures are retrieved from the two previous worksheets and from individual budgets.

Figures are projected for each month, reflecting the flow of cash in and out of your business for a one-year period. Begin with the first month of your business cycle and proceed as follows:

1. Project the Beginning Cash Balance. Enter under "January."
2. Project the Cash Receipts for January. Apportion your total year's revenues throughout the 12 months. Try to weigh revenues as closely as you can to a realistic selling cycle for your industry.
3. Add Beginning Cash Balance and Cash Receipts to determine Total Cash Available.
4. Project cash payments to be made for cost of goods to be sold (inventory that you will purchase or manufacture). Apportion your total inventory budget throughout the year, being sure you are providing for levels of inventory that will fulfill your needs for sales projected.
5. Customize your Variable and Fixed Expense categories to match your business.
6. Project Variable, Fixed, and Interest Expenses for January. Fill out any that you can for all 12 months.
7. Project cash to be paid out on Taxes, Long-Term Assets, Loan Repayments and Owner Draws.
8. Calculate Total Cash Paid Out (Total of Cost of Goods to Be Sold, Variable, Fixed, Interest, Taxes, Long-Term Asset payments, Loan Repayments, and Owner Draws).
9. Subtract Total Cash Paid Out from Total Cash Available. The result is entered under "Cash Balance/Deficiency." Be sure to bracket this figure if the result is a negative to avoid errors.
10. Look at Ending Cash Balance in each of the months and project Loans to be Received and Equity Deposits to be made. Add to Cash Balance/Deficiency to arrive at Ending Cash Balance for each month.
11. Ending Cash Balance for January is carried forward and becomes February's Beginning Cash Balance as throughout the spreadsheet. (Each month's ending balance is the next month's beginning balance.)
12. Go to February and input any numbers that are still needed to complete that month. The process is repeated until December is completed.

To Complete the "Total" Column

1. The Beginning Cash Balance for January is entered in the first space of the "Total" column.
2. The monthly figures for each category (except Beginning Cash Balance, Total Cash Available, Cash Balance/Deficiency, and Ending Cash Balance) are added horizontally and the result entered in the corresponding Total category.
3. The Total column is then computed in the same manner as each of the individual months. If you have been accurate, your computations, the December Ending Cash Balance will be exactly the same as the Total Ending Cash Balance.

Note: If your business is new, you will have to base your projections solely on market research and industry trends. If you have an established business, you will also use your financial statements from previous years. This process may seem complicated, but as you work with it, it will begin to make perfect sense and will be a straightforward and reasonable task to accomplish.

Ace Sporting Goods
Pro Forma Cash Flow Statement

This is the full extension of the previous form (partial cash flow statement). There is a blank form in the Appendix for your use.

Year: ____	Jan	Feb	Mar	Apr	May	Jun	6-MONTH TOTALS	Jul	Aug	Sep	Oct	Nov	Dec	12-MONTH TOTALS
BEGINNING CASH BALANCE														
CASH RECEIPTS														
A. Sales/revenues (cash sales)														
B. Receivables to be collected														
C. Interest income														
D. Sale of long-term assets														
TOTAL CASH AVAILABLE														
CASH PAYMENTS														
A. Cost of goods to be sold														
1. Purchases														
2. Material														
3. Labor														
Total cost of goods														
B. Variable expenses (selling)														
1. Advertising/marketing														
2. Event planning														
3. Freight														
4. Sales salaries														
5. Travel														
6. Vehicle														
7. Misc. selling expense														
Total variable expenses														
C. Fixed expenses (admin.)														
1. Financial administration														
2. Insurance														
3. Licenses and permits														
4. Office salaries														
5. Rent expense														
6. Utilities														
7. Misc. administrative expense														
Total fixed expenses														
D. Interest expense														
E. Federal income tax														
F. Other uses														
G. Long-term asset payments														
H. Loan payments														
I. Owner draws														
TOTAL CASH PAID OUT														
CASH BALANCE/DEFICIENCY														
LOANS TO BE RECEIVED														
EQUITY DEPOSITS														
ENDING CASH BALANCE														

Developing a Marketing Plan

In Chapter 3, you researched your market and now have a good idea of the composition of your customer base or target market. You checked out the competition and have a good understanding of your industry. You determined the best way to reach your market. The development of a marketing plan builds on this information. Look at what are called the "4 P's" of marketing. This analysis will help develop the focus needed to determine your business objectives.

❖ ❖ ❖ ❖ ❖

Over 40 years ago, Neil Borden introduced the concept of the 4 P's that have become the basis of traditional marketing. Basically, the concept involves **product**, **place**, **price**, and **promotion**. Take a look at these topics before moving into the development of the marketing plan. As you will see, they each play a role in how strategies and tactics will be developed.

Product or Service

The first "P" stands for product or service. Basic to marketing is a clear understanding of your product or service and the unique considerations inherent in their differences. A product is a physical and tangible thing. It can be seen and touched. When you buy it, you own it. What you buy is what you get! A service is a task provided by one party for another. It is not tangible, it cannot be seen or touched, and you do not "own" it. Products are usually produced and then sold. By contrast, services are often sold first and then produced or performed. Products can be produced and stored as inventory; services can't be stored and this can create a challenge in anticipating supply and demand.

Business owners generally think in terms of developing an individual product or service when starting a new business. You may have more success in reaching your customers by also providing related products or services. It is important to listen to your target market. Find out what they want and develop a product or service line to meet their needs. For example, the marketing research for Ace Sporting Goods indicated that customers wanted to try equipment before purchase. Providing an area of the store where golf clubs and putters can be safely tested would be a service that could lead to a product sale. This decision is in response to customer feedback.

Throughout your marketing experience, you will hear the term **positioning**. A product or service position is determined by the image projected in terms of the competition, pricing, packaging, distribution, location, and timing of market entry. Your market research will have given you insights into the ways in which to position your product or service. You know your competition, how they advertise and who they serve. You have compared the pricing structures, the distribution channels, the packaging, and the location of the competitors. Positioning is much like a ranking system. Determine where you want to be on the ladder. Choose the most effective combination of products and/or services to offer as a product line based on feedback from your customers. Determine where you want your product line to be positioned in the marketplace. For example, Ace Sporting Goods is positioning itself to be the premier sporting goods store in the county that stocks and specializes in fishing equipment. It is also the only store to provide an area for viewing sport instructional videos.

As you develop your product or service, never lose sight of the needs and preferences of your customers. If their expectations are not met, you will lose their interest in purchasing your product or using your service.

Place

The second "P" stands for place. It refers to the decisions a company makes to ensure that a product or service gets to the customer at the right location and in the right manner. Place can also be expanded to include methods of distribution as well as your business location. Location was discussed in detail in Chapter 5.

Distribution is a major component of the marketing mix. The distribution process has been compared to a pipeline or channel. Information, orders, products, services, and payments flow from consumer to product manufacturer or service provider and back again. What is the normal process for order placement and delivery in the business you are developing? What are the cost factors such as commissions, delivery, shipping fees, and warehousing involved? Develop a flow chart for your product from inventory to sale to delivery and look at the time and costs involved in the process.

For example, the primary location for Ace Sporting Goods will be a retail store in Blair, NY. Sports products will be ordered from manufacturers and wholesalers at a discounted price and will be shipped to the store where they will be put into inventory until sold. Products can also be distributed through other methods. Fly-fishing classes will be taught off-site in order to better reach the market. Product will be pre-sold at time of class registration and will be delivered to the class. The store may wish to develop mail-order sales or an electronic virtual catalog. All are ways of distributing products from one location.

Price

The third "P" is pricing. Pricing is also a marketing decision, combining market research with financial analysis. To be successful, a business owner must establish prices for goods and services that will allow for a profit margin, will be competitive with similar businesses, and will be acceptable to the customer. Pricing can "make or break" a business. If the price is wrong, it won't matter that everything else is right.

One of the problems we have as business owners is that we price a product or service at what we **want** it to sell for, rather than at what it **will** sell for. There are two important factors to keep in mind when developing a pricing structure.

1. *Price ceiling.* You will need to determine the price ceiling; this is the most a customer will pay for your product or service. It is "what the traffic will bear." This is the customer's perception of what you have to offer and, often, this amount has been set by the competition. The customers are used to paying a certain dollar amount. Market research will help you arrive at that figure. Your questionnaires and interview feedback will show what a customer will expect to pay. The information from trade and professional associations will indicate pricing trends and guidelines. The principle to remember is that products or services are bought on the basis of perceived value in the minds of buyers, not on the basis of what it costs you to produce or purchase a product or to provide a service. For example, the **Market Research Worksheet for Ace Sporting Goods** indicated that the market would only pay $55 for a ten-hour guided trip to the Carson River.

2. *Price floor.* Even though the cost of your product or service is not directly related to what the customer is willing to pay for it, costs are of extreme importance to you as the business owner. You must

be aware of how much it cost you to produce your product or provide your service. This means you must take into account all of the operating and other expenses of the business. Evaluation of your costs and expenses allows you to establish a price floor, the price below which you cannot sell and make the necessary profit. The owner of Ace Sporting Goods looked at all of the costs involved in putting his Carson River fishing trip together and determined that ten participants were needed to break-even. Fewer attendees would result in a loss; more attendees would mean a profit.

Successful businesses operate between their price floor and price ceiling.

Promotion

The fourth "P" stands for promotion and involves using the most cost-effective and appropriate promotional methods to enable you to attract customers, to make sales, and keep repeat customers. Chapter 19, "Promoting your Business," is devoted to covering ways in which to promote and advertise your business.

Marketing is primarily what you do **before** and **after** the sale. It is everything you do to make the first sale possible and to make a repeat sale likely. A marketing plan is a key component in the development of a business. It is an organized system for setting up a process for reaching your market and involves determining **objectives**, developing a **strategy** for reaching those objectives, implementing the strategy through various **tactics**, and setting up an **evaluation** process to make sure your plan is working.

Determining Your Objectives

Step one involves identifying what you hope to accomplish. You have a fairly clear vision of what you want your business to be in terms of its size, service or product provided, and market to be served. Express that vision as specific, quantifiable goals and objectives. Being specific is the only way to realistically focus your business and your marketing activities.

For new businesses, this may be attaining a certain sales volume or capturing a certain share of the market. Do you want to gross $60,000 during the first year of operation for Ace Sporting Goods? Do you want to capture 10 percent of the market for take-out food in your geographical area? Objectives can be formed for many aspects of your business. You may want to increase your customer base, set a goal of hiring five new employees, create three new jobs, develop a customer satisfaction program, or market on the Internet. A **Marketing Action Plan for Ace Sporting Goods** has been included on page 181 as an example.

Developing a Strategy

With your goals in mind, you want to decide on overall marketing approaches for each of your products or services and for your business. A marketing strategy is the general method you will use to achieve a goal.

Once you have identified objectives and know what you want your business to accomplish, you are ready to develop a strategy for achieving those objectives. A marketing strategy is a game plan for getting products and services into the hands of your customers in a timely, cost-effective, and appropriate manner.

Tactics for Implementing a Strategy

A marketing tactic is a specific method or program you develop and implement for carrying out the strategy and quantifies the desired result. Tactics are the day-to-day actions you take to put your plan strategy into action. Use the information you developed when you worked through the four "Ps." What **promotion** will work best for implementing your strategy? If you use a delivery truck as part of your distribution (**place**), signage on the truck can make your business visible. Have you considered discount coupons as part of your **pricing** plan?

Deciding on your strategies and tactics will involve looking at what you can afford to spend, what is appropriate for your particular market, product, or service, and what is likely to reach your market in the most effective way.

Evaluating the Results

To be of value, you must develop a plan for evaluating the results. If your objective was to increase revenue by 20 percent in six months, did your sales figures show the desired increase? What did it cost you to reach this goal? Was it cost-effective?

If your objectives are being met, it can mean that your strategy has been successful. You may want to continue with the same tactics. Remember that markets are dynamic and that what works now may not work in the future. Also, different markets react to different tactics. Successful businesses conduct on-going market research throughout the life of their business. They do customer surveys, keep up with industry changes, and keep track of population changes in their target areas.

If your objectives haven't been met, look closely at your tactics. You may have to revise your plan of attack. Do more of what works and eliminate that which didn't produce the desired results.

After you have been in business for awhile, your financial statements will give a clear picture of how your business has performed financially. By comparing actual results with your objectives over a period of time, you can identify what is working and what is not. Your marketing plan is like a game plan. Basic market research and previous results are used by businesses to set new objectives and begin the cycle over again.

Marketing Action Plan
for Ace Sporting Goods

Objective	Strategy	Tactic	Evaluation
Increase revenue from Carson River trips	Offer Carson River trips twice per month during fishing season. Each trip participation needs 24 people with three guides.	Increase awareness of fly-fishing through: • in-store demos • in-store viewing of fly-fishing videotapes • press releases • bi-monthly drawing for one free trip • direct mail to drawing participants.	Keep track of sign-up at in-store demos. Monitor interest from press releases. Keep track of participation in drawing.
Increase sales of sporting goods equipment in store.	Acquire new customers. Encourage repeat business.	Hold a grand opening Run ads in local newspaper. Saturate surrounding area with 10 percent off coupons valid during first week of operation. Give additional discount coupon to all customers who make a purchase during first week of operation	Keep track of percent of sales coming from advertising. Keep track of percent of sales coming from coupons. Keep track of percent of first-time customers who return.

Promoting Your Business

Advertising is the means for getting information about your product or service to the buying public. The first step in developing an advertising plan is to define potential customers in the geographic area served by your business. Do some preliminary surveys and interviews to determine which means of advertising will reach them. What newspapers do they read? Which radio stations do they listen to? Do they use discount coupons? Do they respond to direct mail? Do they have access to the Internet? Tailor your advertising efforts to your market.

◆ ◆ ◆ ◆

By now you will have identified what is **unique** about your business and how that uniqueness will **benefit the customer**. This theme or image for your product or service should carry through all of your advertising. It is what sets you apart from the competition and it is what will attract the customer.

When you know which audience you want to target, where they are located, and what you want to tell them, it is time to look at how you will reach them. There are a variety of ways to accomplish this through the media, with publicity and by alternative methods of advertising.

Media Advertising

Media advertising and publicity can be obtained through interviews, articles, and paid advertisements in newspapers, magazines, on radio, and on television.

Publicity: any non-paid, news-oriented presentation of a product, service or business entity in a mass media format.

Newspaper advertising. This form of publicity usually reaches a large audience, has a short life span, is relatively inexpensive, and is quickly and easily changed. Tailor your ad to the editorial "mood" of the paper. Determine what special feature sections are being planned by calling the newspaper's editorial staff. If the paper is planning to do a special feature on "desktop publishing" and you will be opening a mobile repair service for such equipment, you may want to advertise in that section. Your ad can be placed to reach a selected audience; the people reading that section will be interested in desktop publishing and in your business. The cost of the ad will vary according to frequency of publication and area of circulation. Ads are available in various sizes and in several formats such as display or classified ads. Analyze the advertising of your competition regarding size, placement, and frequency. Your questionnaires and market research will have indicated the newspapers read by your target market. Those are the papers in which you will place your advertising.

Magazine advertising. This is often overlooked by small business owners because ads are thought to be too costly to prepare and run. You don't have to run your ad in the entire edition of a magazine. You can reach specific geographic and demographic markets by placing your ad in a regional edition. The directories published by Standard Rate and Data Service are available in your library and will tell you which magazines have regional editions and how much they charge for advertising space. You may also cut down your cost by making use of "remnant space." Often a magazine will not have sold all of its advertising space prior to press time. These remnant spaces are often sold at a deep discount in order to fill the page. Contact the publication well in advance of the date when you wish your ad to appear and determine their policies. Some magazines will provide extra services such as reader response cards that enable you to develop a mailing list of individuals interested in what you have to offer.

One of the disadvantages of magazine advertising is that your ad must be placed well in advance of the issue's publication, which does not allow for last minute changes. You also have very little control over where your ad will appear in the magazine. Expensive items generally do not sell well through magazine ads. This type of advertising is best suited for mail-order businesses and name brand merchandise.

Brand: a design, mark, symbol or other device that distinguishes one line or type of goods from those of a competitor.

Magazine ads carry a large degree of credibility and prestige and are worth considering as an advertising option.

Radio advertising. Advertising by radio is usually local, reaches a preselected audience, can be changed frequently, is limited to brief copy, is relatively expensive, and can be repeated frequently. It is priced according to length of message, time of broadcast, and frequency of broadcast. It is either read live by broadcasters or taped in advance.

There are two types of radio programming: background and foreground. Background programs are on the music stations. Foreground programs are on the news/talk stations. Foreground programs involve more active listeners who will probably pay more attention to your commercials.

It has been proven that you must catch the listener's attention in the first three seconds. Your ad will be done live or taped in advance. The three biggest complaints about radio commercials are that they are noisy, they have inane humor, and they lack sincerity. Keep that in mind if you write your own commercial. Be simple and straightforward. Another approach to radio coverage of your business would be to offer your service as an expert in your field on a radio talk show. You can answer questions from listeners and tell about your business.

Television advertising. This medium reaches large marketing areas, is relatively expensive, and is limited to brief copy. This form of advertising is usually highly professional and is priced according to length of message, time of broadcast, frequency of broadcast, time of year, and whether the station is an independent or a member of a network.

Cost of advertising is based on gross rating points (GRP). One point equals one percent of the television sets in the TV marketing area. The GRP unit cost is determined by the competitive situation, size of area, and time of year. Advertising costs may be higher during the holiday season, which is considered to be October through December. Prime time covers the period from 8:00 to 11:00 PM and is more costly. The "fringe time" before and after prime time may be more cost-effective for you. Don't discount cable television. This medium is becoming very useful to the small business owner. In many communities, low cost seminars are presented to instruct you in developing your own cable television ads or programs.

You need to know which media are most likely to influence your target audience and which reporters cover your kind of business. The public library has media source books available that list newspapers, magazines, radio, and television stations. Find out what shows your customers watch. Television stations will have demographic and psychographic breakdowns of their viewing audiences. Most use market studies to effectively help position advertising where it will be seen by those interested in the products or services offered.

Advertising takes planning, time, persistence, and money. The true effectiveness of advertising is measured over time. Your target market must be repeatedly reminded of the benefits of doing business with you. This repetition has a cumulative effect. Customers will see you as an established business. Use the **Advertising Worksheet** on page 194 as you plan which types of advertising methods will be used, how much they will cost, and when they will be used. The planning process is like drawing a blueprint. First design the framework, next fill in the details, and then begin to build the advertising plan.

Publicity

In addition to paid advertising, don't overlook publicity. Publicity has been defined as "free advertising." Research print media, television, and radio stations in your area with the help of your local library. Media references available in the library will provide you with a listing of sources and contact names. Call programmers for the radio and television talk programs and editors of the newspapers and magazines in your area. Ask if they will be doing a feature on your area of expertise. If they are, offer your services as an expert working in that field. You may be interviewed and profiled, you may be able to submit an article for publication or you may wish to place some targeted advertising to coincide with the feature. If no feature is being planned, explain why this would be a timely topic and would be of interest to their audiences.

It is not enough to just tell about your business. You must be prepared to present a unique angle. You must convince the editor or programmer that what you have to say will appeal and will be of interest to their readers, listeners, and viewers. The information you submit and the ideas you approach the media with must be timely, important, and interesting to a large segment of their audience.

You may wish to submit a **news release** in order to let people know who you are and what you have to offer. When preparing a press release, the two primary concerns are content and structure. News releases should be as short as possible while containing all of the important facts. Make every effort to write it in good journalistic style. Read news releases in your target news outlets and study format and content. News writing follows the "inverted pyramid" style in which every paragraph is considered more important than the ones following it. The story is written in descending order of importance. That means the news is up front. A busy reader whose interest is not caught in the first paragraph will not read the second one. **News Release Information**, a **News Release Format** sheet and a **Sample News Release** are included on pages 195, 196, and 197, respectively.

Alternative Methods

In addition to advertising and publicity, there are other means of getting the message about your business to your customers. **Displays** may be set up at community-oriented functions such as city fairs, community events, and civic meetings. This is a good way to present your product or service to the buying public. You can also get valuable feedback. **Community involvement** can be an effective means of advertising. Membership in civic organizations can pave the way to being a guest speaker. Active membership affords you the opportunity for networking. **Networking** is the exchange of ideas and information that takes place everyday in your life. You are going to direct that exchange to your benefit and to the benefit of those around you. The more you meet with people, the more you will be able to promote your business, to learn more about the business community around you, and to become more self-confident. Membership in civic and business organizations such as the chamber of commerce is an excellent means of accomplishing this.

Trade show and **exhibit** participation allows you to take advantage of promotional campaigns that would be too expensive for a small business to undertake alone. You can request listings of trade events from malls and convention centers. Participation in trade shows and membership in trade organizations give you visibility in your business field. These shows are usually attended only by those interested in your particular field. This is an excellent way to reach your target market. You may choose to participate in a co-op display to cut costs.

Direct mail. This is an effective way to deliver specific information in a personal way to large numbers of people. Direct mail can take the form of inexpensive fact sheets, letters, promotional give-aways, contests, discount coupons, and brochures. It can be used to solicit mail-order or phone-order business, to announce new products or services, to notify customers of price changes, to welcome new customers, to thank current customers, and to announce special events such as sales. To be cost-effective, you must target your market. Rent a good list from a list broker.

Direct mail: marketing goods or services directly to the consumer through the mail.

TECH TIP 20
Direct E-Mail

Ask potential and existing customers for their e-mail addresses and for permission to provide them with information. Send them industry news, monthly product updates, announcements of special sales, and hyperlinks to your Web site and to other sites of interest. Encourage them to bookmark your Web site; let them know you frequently update the site and provide timely and useful information that will benefit them. This is the fastest, most cost-effective, cutting edge method for reaching customers.

Telemarketing. This form of promotion can be an effective method for reaching your customers. The telephone can be used to contact new customers, to maintain contact with current clients, and to prod slow payers with a personal reminder. Telephone selling is well established in business-to-business marketing. Telemarketing from business to consumer is most effective when the business owner has carefully researched the demographics and psychographics of the customer base. Individuals who commute alone more than 35 minutes one way, have a tape deck in their vehicles, and belong to health clubs are more likely to be interested in your 25 minute "Exercise While Driving" tape than residents of a retirement community! Targeted mailing lists can be rented which include telephone numbers.

We all experience what is termed "call reluctance" and even professionals admit that "cold calling" can be intimidating. You can conquer this reluctance and fear by developing a strategy. To be effective, telemarketing must be organized. Develop a script or outline of the key points of your offer, prepare answers to what you perceive will be the most-asked questions, practice your delivery, or recruit and train people capable of making a professional presentation. Professional firms can be hired to conduct your telemarketing campaign.

Many companies are finding it effective to send an introductory mailing which is followed by a "warm call."

- ◆ Determine the key decision maker you want to reach.
- ◆ Send an introductory letter, sample, or offer.
- ◆ Call within one week of receipt of the mailing. (Your post office can give you an estimation of delivery time.)
- ◆ If you get a positive response, close the deal and send a "thank you" message.
- ◆ If you get a negative response, send a "thank you" note indicating your appreciation for their time and letting them know your company may be able to meet their needs at some future time.

This strategy allows you to combine telemarketing with direct mail and gives you the opportunity to present your business three times.

Yellow Page listings. Listings are an effective means of advertising. Every person with a phone has a copy of the Yellow Pages. You have a captive audience; they are looking at the directory because they are interested in what you have to offer. This is the most widely used form of advertising. One business owner states that in any given week, 50 percent of her customers are directed to her clock repair shop through her Yellow Pages ad.

TECH TIP 21
Downloadable Discounts

You can publish coupons on your Web site that can be downloaded and printed. Your site can let customers know these coupons are only available at the site and encourage your customers to bring them to your store for a discount. This is a good way to track the type of customers who are accessing your site and the frequency of their return to the site.

The telephone company advertising staff is very knowledgeable and will give you help in designing an ad that will present your business in an effective manner. Be aware that directories are published at various times of the year. Call the phone company to determine publication deadlines.

Discounts. This is another way to get additional customers. Discounts can be given to new customers and to customers who bring in referrals. They may also be offered through coupons and brochures. Everyone likes to think that they are saving money.

Promotional gimmicks. T-shirts, pens, key rings, plastic shopping bags, calendars, balloons, and bumper stickers can also get your name in front of the public. The most effective promotional materials are useful items. They should be appropriate to the business that they represent. For example, a logo or business name on a T-shirt is an effective way of advertising a business dealing with the out-of-doors, such as a bicycle shop or a kite maker. Pens would be a good item for a manufacturer of note cards and stationery. Balloons could represent a company specializing in children's items. Be creative in your use of this advertising form.

Customer contact. Contact with your customers has never been easier. New technology enables you to develop a computer database of your customer files. A tickler file can be set up to alert you to special events in the lives of your customers; birthday cards, discount coupons, industry news can be sent via regular or electronic mail. An 800-phone number makes it easy for customers to reach you at no cost to them. Cellular phones and pagers enable you, the business owner, to be in contact with your market at all times wherever you may be and allows you to respond immediately. No matter what type of business you are in, technology can enable you to work more efficiently, to better meet the needs of your customer base, and to increase your profits.

Home page: the "table of contents" to a Web site, detailing what pages are on a particular site. The first page one sees when accessing a Web site.

Marketing on the Internet

Technology is affecting virtually every business. People go on the World Wide Web (www) for a variety of reasons; they conduct research, they communicate via electronic mail (e-mail), they seek out education and training sites, and they make purchases (e-commerce). Many companies are rushing to develop Web sites and to put their brochures and catalogs online so customers can browse, select products, ask questions, and place orders through their home or office computers. This technology has opened up many new marketing opportunities for businesses.

A business can set up a virtual storefront and market its products and services through a Web site located on the Internet. The Internet has been described as "the Yellow Pages of cyberspace." Consumers surf the Web looking for products and services they need. Before deciding on the value of a Web site for your business, answer the following questions:

◆ *Why do you need a Web site?* Before investing time and money into the development of your site, answer a few questions. Is your competition marketing over the Internet? To remain competitive, do you also need a presence? Look at their Web site and evaluate it. Do you want to expand geographically? Marketing on the Internet will allow your marketing materials to be viewed internationally. Are you ready for such wide exposure? If you want to remain fairly local, link up with a local identity for inclusion of your Web page. For example, many chambers of commerce are hosting sites that include information on local businesses.

◆ *What do you hope to accomplish through your site?* Do you want to provide information? Do you want an interactive site so you can gather information from your customers? Do you want to make sales? If so, how are you going to be paid? If you are going to take orders online, you will need to establish a secure server. This is technology that will encrypt or code your customers' credit card information so they may complete payment for the transaction over the Internet.

◆ *Who will be accessing your material?* Do your potential or existing customers own computers? Do they have modems and online services? Do they purchase over the Internet? Make sure the market you have researched and that you intend to reach is available through this medium.

◆ *How will they reach your site?* Will individuals just stumble upon your site or do you have a plan for leading them to it? Your Web site must be on all of your marketing materials and listed in all directories. When composing your Web pages, use words or terms that your potential customers might use when searching for your product or service.

TECH TIP 22
Electronic Commerce (E-Commerce)

Sales transactions over the Internet are referred to as e-commerce. This is one of the fastest growing areas of Internet use. Customers view catalog-like Web pages, select the items they wish to order, add them to a "shopping basket," and key in personal information on an interactive order form. The customer's credit card information is kept secure by encrypted software as it is transferred via modem to your computer. This medium allows you to capture the customer's e-mail address for future promotions, shipping address for tracking response geographically, and demographic information for analysis of the segment of your market that shops over the Internet.

The following sites provide additional information on this subject:

www.zdnet.com/
Search "e-commerce" from the home page to access the magazine archives that contain articles on e-commerce. This site provides numerous links to information sources on this topic.

www.efuse.com/Plan/e-commerce_basics.html
This site provides an excellent overview of e-commerce with links to additional information.

To view examples of effective, interactive Web pages, access the following sites:

www.jellybelly.com
www.ragu.com

Note that the use of the company's name as the domain name enables the customer to remember the site. The Jelly Belly site enables the user to order online, find a local retailer, download recipes, and learn about special events. By filling out a questionnaire, the user can receive a free sample. This interactive site allows the company to track product interest geographically for future retail placement. The Ragu site provides recipes and a chat "dining" room complete with Italian lessons. While these sites are very expensive to develop, monitor, and maintain, they illustrate what can be done to capture and keep a customer's interest. These sites are changed frequently to keep customers coming back.

Even though your initial research may indicate your market is not now computerized, does not order via the Internet, or would not expect to find you on this medium, markets change. Keep up-to-date on new technology and the changing marketplace.

About Web Pages

Like the Yellow Pages and other directories, consumers don't want to spend a lot of time reading detailed text. A well-designed Web site can capture the interest of a potential customer and keep an existing customer returning to your site. Following are some considerations when developing your Web site:

◆ *Be consistent.* Just like your other promotional materials, your Web site must project your company's image.

♦ *Keep it simple.* You have 15 seconds to capture the customer's interest. The text should be simple and easy to read. Avoid an abundance of graphics; the page will take too long to come up on the screen and your customers will move on before your message can be fully viewed. Use a background color that does not compete with or drown out the information.

♦ *Be information-based.* Potential customers have come to your site to find out about your product or service. Give them the information they need in as short a time as possible.

♦ *Make navigation easy.* Develop a home page with icons that can be clicked on to go to subsequent pages with additional information. The home page of Ace Sporting Goods would briefly give information regarding the nature of the business, the e-mail address, 800-phone number, and address. Icons would be included for sporting goods categories. Separate icons could be included for in-store programs and special sales. If a potential or existing customer was only interested in fly-fishing, a few clicks would take that customer to a listing of equipment for sale, special promotions, and in-store programs. The customer would not have to wade through baseball, golf, and tennis information.

Contact your nearest Small Business Administration office, Small Business Development Center, or local college to find out about low-cost workshops and seminars on the subjects of the Internet marketing and Web page development. Your decision to market in this medium should be an educated one.

Summary

In summary, pay attention to advertising and promotions that attract your attention. Try to analyze successful advertising done by professionals for tips on designing your own ads. Your advertising should be the highest quality you can afford and as professional as possible. Your advertising represents you and your business and conveys an impression to the public.

All promotion costs something. Advertising is a necessary expense for establishing, maintaining, and expanding your business. Deciding how much money to spend to advertise your product or service can be difficult. The size of your advertising budget should be determined by long-range as well as immediate sales objectives. Although the proportion of income spent on advertising varies according to the type of business, the average is 1.5 percent. The Small Business Administration suggests that it is not the amount that is spent but how it is spent that counts. The rule of thumb is that the cost of advertising must be offset by the increase in its resulting profits. View advertising costs as an investment in your company's future and choose the methods that will best reach your target market. Advertising must be cost-effective.

All forms of advertising and publicity must be evaluated for effectiveness. To help you with this analysis, an **Advertising Response Record** and a **Publicity Tracking Record** have been included on pages 198 and 199. From this information, determine which form of advertising has worked best for your business. Eliminate those methods that have not proven effective and transfer those funds to a more productive area. After evaluating the different methods of advertising, work up an individual plan for your business.

Advertising Worksheet

Name of business: __Ace Sporting Goods__

1. What are the features and benefits of my product or service? __Knowledgeable trained staff;__ __open until 9 PM weekdays, 1-5 PM Sunday; full sports product line, specializing__ __in fishing gear; offer fly-tying and fly-fishing classes; in-house guarantee of sports__ __equipment.__

2. Who is my audience? _____
   __Youth, high school, university students__
   __Active, middle-income sports enthusiasts__
   __Live within ten-mile radius__

3. Who is my competition and how do they advertise? _____
   __Smith Sporting Goods—radio ads KLXY__
   __Mailing of flyers—newspaper ad—Sunday supplement__
   __Promotions—caps, T-shirts__

4. What are the goals of my advertising campaign? _____
   __Reach high school and university market.__
   __Reach youth market.__
   __Reach fishing enthusiasts.__

5. How much do I plan to invest for advertising? __$1,300 per month__
   _____
   _____
   _____
   _____

6. What advertising methods will I use? _____

_x_ Newspapers	__ Magazines	_x_ Yellow Pages
__ Radio	__ Television	_x_ Direct mail
__ Telemarketing	_x_ Flyers	__ Brochures
_x_ Coupons	__ Press release	_x_ Promo items
_x_ Other __youth team sponsorship__		

7. When will I use them and what will they cost? _____
   Newspaper: start 1/3/00 weekly ad x 5 $300/mo.
   Direct mail flyers: 1/7/00 and 1/14/00 $550 total
   Youth team: 1/26/00 $150/mo.
   Promo items: 1/16/00 $100/mo.
   Yellow Page ad: 1/25/00 (March directory) $200/mo.

8. How will I measure the effectiveness of the advertising plan? _____
   a. Ask customers how they heard about the store.
   b. Compare cost/income on Advertising Response Record.
      1. Change or delete methods that cost more than income generated.
      2. Adjust or increase budget to include radio ad, brochure, larger Yellow Page
         and newspaper ads.

News Release Information

Identification

The business sending the release should be plainly identified. Use your letterhead or printed news release forms. The name and telephone number of a contact person for additional information must appear at the top of the page.

Release date

Most releases should be "immediate" or "for use upon receipt." Designate a release time only if there is a specific reason, such as a scheduled speech, meeting, news announcement, or planned event.

Margins

Leave wide margins and space at the top so the editor can edit and include notations.

Headlines

The headline you submit should be to summarize your writing. The media will generally create their own headline.

Length

Most press releases are one page in length. If you have a longer release, write the highlights into an attached news memo and include the news release as background material.

Style

Use the summary lead and the five Ws (who, what, when, where, why, and, sometimes, how). Double-space. Use short sentences with active verbs. Make sure it is accurate, timely, and not self-serving. Try to use an objective style of writing. If you must use more than one page, do not split a paragraph from the first to second page. Center the word "more" at the bottom of the first page.

Check and Doublecheck

Proofread names, spellings, numbers, and grammar carefully.

Placement

Your news release should be in the hands of editors well in advance of deadlines. Contact the city desk, assignment editor, or feature editor with whom you are working to clarify deadlines and publication schedules.

End

Put "30" or ### at the end of the press release.

News releases should be cleanly typed on 8½ x 11-inch white paper. They should be hand-delivered or mailed first-class to the designated media contact.

News Release Format

(Print on Company Letterhead or News Memo Form)

TO: Addressed to editor or reporter

FROM: Your name, address, and phone number.

RE: A one or two sentence statement regarding the story you are suggesting, the event to which you are inviting reporters, the meeting, class or seminar you have scheduled, or other purpose of the news release.

TIME AND DATE: Specific time, date, year of event, or of submission release.

LOCATION: Specific location, including directions if the location is not well-known or easily found.

WHY: You must have a reason for the news release or the event.

CONTACT: The name and phone number of someone the news editor or reporters can contact with questions about the news release.

Sample News Release

(Print on Company Letterhead or Press Release Form)

PRESS RELEASE

September 6, 2000   Contact: David Blair

For Immediate Release   (555) 613-7965

Fly-Fishing Demonstration and Contest

John Bacon, well-known local fly-fisherman, will demonstrate techniques for dry and wet fly casting and will judge a contest to be held in the parking lot of Ace Sporting Goods on Saturday, September 26, 2000 from 10 AM to 4 PM.

Ace's owner, David Blair, stated that the popularity of the book and movie, *A River Runs Through It*, has led to an increased interest in the sport of fly-fishing. Blair announced that the fee for participation in the contest is $5 with all of the proceeds going to the Memorial Hospital Children's Wing. All contestants will receive a ten percent discount coupon from the sporting goods store.

After receiving instructions from Mr. Bacon, contestants will be judged on form, distance, and accuracy. Prizes include theater passes, dinner coupons, and sporting event tickets. The contest is open to everyone. Information and pre-registration are available at Ace Sporting Goods, 271 Adams St., Blair, NY or by phoning (555) 613-7965.

-30-

Advertising Response Record

Company name: Ace Sporting Goods—January 2000

Type of Ad	Date Run	Cost	Circulation	Number of Responses	Income Generated
Register newspaper 2" x 4" in sports section	Weekly 1/3, 1/10, 1/17, 1/24, 1/31	$300.00	15,000	end of month coupon responses—264 phone orders—26	$6,600.00 $520.00
Flyers with 10% discount coupon—high school, university	Mailed 1/7/00	$350.00	750	10	$260.00
Flyers with 10% discount for fishermen	Mailed 1/14/00	$200.00	500	96	$1,152.00
Youth team sponsorship caps/shirts with store name	1/26/00	$150.00	12	6 team members purchased equipment at 20% discount	$135.00

In this example, the newspaper ad, which included the ten percent off coupon generated income of $7,120 with an expense of $300. By analyzing the response to newspaper advertising over time, the owner of Ace Sporting Goods can determine whether the initial interest was due to curiosity about a new store or whether there is continued response to this form of advertising. The discount flyers mailed to the high school and university students were not cost-effective. The flyers mailed to a targeted mailing list of fishermen was more effective: at a cost of $200, 96 new customers responded and spent $1,152. The sponsorship of a youth sports team may appear to lose money, but the goodwill and visibility generated is worth the small loss. The response to your advertising must be analyzed throughout the lifetime of a business. This type of analysis will help you determine the most effective use of your advertising dollars.

Publicity Tracking Record

Company name: _Ace Sporting Goods_

Media Name	Contact Person	Address	Date	Material Sent	Follow-up	Response	Results	Notes
KRTZ Radio "News About Town"	Jim Bell, Prog. Dir, 555-8120	722 Main Baker, MD 20601	9/9/00	News Memo Promo Kit	9/16 phoned	9/18 booked for 10/2 talk show 7–8 PM	15 calls taken on air 160 requests for brochure	Focus: Opening of fishing season. Fly-tying and fishing.
Tribune newspaper	Ann Mead, Sports Ed., 555-6124	621 6th St. Baker, MD 20603	9/10/00	Press Release Promo Kit	9/17 phoned	9/20 submit 500 word article	Article printed 9/27 200 requests for brochure	Focus: Current interest in alternative sport.
Orange City magazine	Karen Brown, Reporter, 555-7093	724 Adams Baker, MD 20603	9/10/00	Promo Kit Photo	10/22 phoned	not interested at this time		Focus: New business opens.
Metro Cable Evening News	David Kim, Prog. Dir, 555-6201	2664 Bryan Baker, MD 20601	10/15/00	Promo Kit Photo		will film fly-tying 6 PM 10/25		Focus: Unique local business.

Evaluating the results of your publicity campaign will help you decide the most effective use of your advertising dollars. The appearance on KRTZ radio netted 15 calls on air and 160 off air requests for brochures. The material sent to listeners should be coded so that responses can be traced. If coupons are used or class registrations taken from this group, you may consider advertising on the station. The same follow-up should be considered with the newspaper article. Although Orange City magazine is not interested at this time, keep in touch and present a new angle at a later date.

Business Planning: The Key to Your Success

The purpose of this chapter is to convince you that you need to write a business plan and to give you some basic information about business planning. We will also provide you with a basic outline listing the components of a well-written plan. If you decide to go ahead with the project (we hope you will!), we have a very comprehensive, step-by-step guide that will take you through the entire process. It is entitled *Anatomy of a Business Plan* (Chicago: Dearborn, 1999). If you are computer-oriented, we have also developed an IBM or compatible software version of the book, complete with word processing and preformatted and preformulated spreadsheets. It is entitled *Automate Your Business Plan* (Out of Your Mind...and Into the Marketplace, Tustin, CA). You can also take classes through most colleges, Small Business Development Centers, or the U.S. Small Business Administration.

❖ ❖ ❖ ❖ ❖

Lack of adequate planning is one of the principal reasons most businesses fail. When the concept of business planning is considered, three critical facts always seem to emerge.

1. All lenders and investors require a business plan.
2. All businesses would operate more profitably with a business plan.
3. Most business owners do not know how to write a winning business plan.

We have been teaching business workshops to entrepreneurs for several years now and have found that no task seems to cause more consternation and dread than that of facing the ominous task of preparing a business plan. In fact, most new business owners will forge ahead being sure that a good idea, enthusiasm, and the desire to achieve their goals will be enough to ensure business success.

Unfortunately, there is a major flaw in this type of thinking. Most business owners are not proficient in all phases of their particular industries and, therefore, do not have enough knowledge to make the best decisions and see what changes will have to be implemented in the future. Business planning is the most effective way to overcome this deficiency and enable you to organize the making of business decisions into a logical process. Most business owners love their business, but hope to avoid anything that resembles paperwork.

You will soon learn that about 20 percent of your time as a business owner will be spent directly working with your product or service. The other 80 percent of the time you will be kept busy doing all of the managerial and miscellaneous chores that need to be done to keep your business functioning.

Why Write a Business Plan?

There are two main purposes for writing a business plan. What are they and why are they important enough to make you decide to write one?

1. *To serve as a guide during the lifetime of your business.* This is the most important reason for writing a business plan. Writing a business plan will force you to consider everything that will come into play to make a success out of your business. It will also provide you with a means to periodically analyze what is happening in your business and give you a solid basis on which to make decisions and implement changes. In short, it is the blueprint of your business and will serve to keep you on the right track. If you will spend the time to plan ahead, many pitfalls will be avoided and needless frustrations will be eliminated.

2. *To fulfill the requirement for securing lenders and investors.* If you are planning to seek loan funds or venture capital, you will be required to submit solid documentation in the form of a business plan.

   The days are gone when your local banker would extend a loan because you are a good trustworthy person with an entrepreneurial idea that sounds great. The world is more complex, competition is keen, and the banker has to have complete documentation that will justify your loan. Remember, a banker is the caretaker of clients' money. If your business plan is realistic and has complete financial documentation that indicates you will be able to repay your loan plus interest, then there is a basis to lend you the funds you need to operate or expand your business. This also applies to venture capitalists who invest in your business in return for a share of the business.

Your business plan will provide potential lenders and investors with detailed information on all aspects of the company's past and current operations and future projections. It will detail how the desired investment or loan will further the company's goals. Every lender and investor wants to know how the loan will improve the worth of your company. Your business plan will detail how the money will be used and how it will enhance the company's profitability.

Revising Your Business Plan

Writing a business plan does not mean you can never vary from that plan. In fact, if your plan is going to be effective either to the business or to a potential lender, it will be necessary for you to update it on a regular basis. Changes are constantly taking place in your industry, in technology, and with your customers. You, as the owner, must be aware of everything that is happening in relation to your business in particular and your industry in general. You must be prepared to take the necessary steps to stay ahead of your competition. Every quarter, you will want to look at what has happened in your business, make decisions about what you can do better, and revise your plan to reflect the changes you want to implement.

Format of a Winning Business Plan

One of the things we also noticed regarding business planning was that most business planning workshops focused heavily on why you should hire a professional planner (usually their company). Since getting into the software business, we have also been confronted with a lot of hype claiming that you can install your business planning software and create a business plan in a few hours.

The fact is that writing a business plan requires many days and possibly months depending on the complexity of your business. But, you can write it yourself—and if you do, you will know your business better before you finish. There is a lot of research to be done. Even if you hire a professional planner, you will be required to supply the information and statistics that will go into your business plan. This phase will be about 80 percent of the job. The other 20 percent is a matter of knowing how to put the information together into a readable plan.

Much of the confusion seems to stem from the fact that most business owners do not know what elements to include or how to organize their information in a logical sequence. As one of our students put it, "If God had boxes of arms, legs, heads, and other parts, and no instructions for putting a human being together, we might be pretty funny looking and not very functional. I think a business plan is the same." He was right. In order to work, a business plan must not only have all of the necessary parts, but be put together in a functional pattern. When you write your business plan, you will want to cover specific subjects in a particular order. You will also need to maintain 100 percent continuity between all sections of the plan. Whatever you document in the text sections must be reflected in the financial documents.

TECH TIP 23

Business Planning Software: Using Technology to Streamline the Process

There is no quick fix when it comes to writing a business plan. However, utilizing the proper tools can make your job easier and save you valuable time. Combining the research capabilities of the Internet and the use of a good business planning software package can help you to create a credible and defensible business plan for your new company.

Unfortunately, in today's world full of over-hyped products, much of the software purchased does not live up to everything promised on the outside of the package. One popular package says on its box front, "Fill in the numbers and write a business plan in a few hours." This should be your clue to run—not walk—to the nearest exit.

**What Should You Look for
in Business Planning Software?**
Remember, your business plan is only as good as the information that you are able to input into the program. It's the old "garbage in—garbage out" adage. Keeping the desired

result in mind, look at software that will enable you to completely customize your business plan to your particular business. This means staying away from templates that create canned plans.

Good software will guide you step-by-step through your business plan, giving you instructions and examples for each piece of your plan, but it will not generate the text for you by having you fill in the blanks. Especially important is your financial plan. Be sure that all of your spreadsheets can be completely customized to your chart of accounts. Generic financial statements will not help you run your business.

We Like Ours Best—of Course!
Automate Your Business Plan for Windows is a companion software to our book, ***Anatomy of a Business Plan***. There are preformatted and preformulated spreadsheets and an International Research Web page. For more information: www.business-plan.com.

Anatomy of a Business Plan Outline

To help make your task easier, we have included a condensed outline (based on our book, *Anatomy of a Business Plan*, and our software, *Automate Your Business Plan*) for you to follow when you write your business plan. Your plan should include all of the elements listed on the next two pages.

Business Plan Outline

adapted from: *Anatomy of a Business Plan*, Fourth Edition
Chicago: Dearborn, 1999
and
Automate Your Business Plan 9.0
Out of Your Mind...and Into the Marketplace, Tustin, CA, 1999

The Cover Sheet

(The title page of your plan.)

The cover sheet should contain the name, address, and telephone number of the business and the names, addresses, and telephone numbers of all owners or corporate officers. It should also tell who prepared the business plan and when the plan was prepared or revised. To help you keep track of copies out to lenders, mark each cover sheet with a copy number.

The Executive Summary

(The thesis statement.)

The Executive Summary summarizes your plan and states your objectives. If you are seeking loan funds or investment capital, it will list your capital needs, how you intend to use the money, the benefit of the loan funds to the business, and how you intend to repay the loan plus interest or return profits to the investor.

While you are writing your plan, many previous ideas will change and new ideas will develop. Therefore, the Executive Summary is most effectively formulated after writing your plan. This summary should be concise and no longer than one page in length.

Table of Contents

(Listing of contents of your plan with page numbers.)

Having a table of contents will help the reader to move smoothly from one section of the plan to another when verifying information.

For example: If a lender is reading financial information regarding advertising on a pro forma cash flow statement, the table of contents will help to locate the advertising section for specifics on where you will be advertising and how the advertising dollars will be spent. The table of contents will also refer to the page in the supporting documents section that will contain advertising rate sheets backing up the advertising plan.

Part I: The Organizational Plan

(The first main section of your business plan.)

This section contains information on how your business is put together administratively. It includes such things as a description of your business, your legal structure, who your management and personnel will be, where you will locate if it is not tied to your marketing, how you will do your accounting, what insurance you will have and what security measures you will take to protect inventory and information.

Part II: The Marketing Plan

(The second main section of your business plan.)

Your marketing plan will contain information on your total market with emphasis on your target market. You will include information on your target market and your competition. You will make such decisions as promotion of your product or service, pricing, timing of market entry, and where to locate if it's tied into your marketing. You will also examine current industry trends.

Part III: Financial Documents

(The third major section of your business plan.)

Your financial documents translate the information in the first two sections of your plan into financial figures that can be used to analyze your business and make decisions for higher profitability.

You will have pro forma (projected) financial statements, actual (historical) statements, and a financial statement analysis. Include a pro forma cash flow statement, three-year income projection, break-even analysis, quarterly budget analysis, profit & loss statement, balance sheet, and a financial statement analysis ratio summary. If you are going to a lender or investor, you will also need a summary of financial needs, loan fund dispersal statement, and a financial history.

Part IV: Supporting Documents

(Documents referred to and used to back up statements made in the three main sections of your business plan.)

This section will include: owner/manager résumés, personal financial statements, articles of incorporation/partnership agreements, legal contracts, lease agreements, proprietary papers (copyrights, trademarks, and patents), letters of reference, demographics, and any other documents which are pertinent to support the plan.

Resources for Small Business

The Small Business Administration

The U.S. Small Business Administration is an independent federal agency created by Congress in 1953 to assist, council, and represent small business. Statistics show that most small business failures are due to poor management. For this reason, the SBA places special emphasis on individual counseling, courses, conferences, workshops, and publications to train the new and existing business owner in all facets of business development with special emphasis on improving the management ability of the owner. Their Web site is: www.sbaonline.sba.gov

Counseling is provided through the Service Corps of Retired Executives (SCORE), Small Business Institutes (SBIs), Small Business Development Centers (SBDCs), and numerous professional associations. The SBA strives to match the need of a specific business with the expertise available.

Business management training covers such topics as planning, finance, organization, and marketing and is held in cooperation with educational institutions, chambers of commerce, and trade associations. Pre-business workshops are held on a regular basis for prospective business owners. Other training programs are conducted that focus on special needs such as rural development, young entrepreneurship, and international trade.

- ◆ **SCORE** is a 13,000-person volunteer program with over 750 locations. SCORE helps small businesses solve their operating problems through free one-on-one counseling and through a well developed system of low-cost workshops and training sessions. To locate a SCORE counseling center in your area or to consult online, access the following site: www.score.org

◈ **Small Business Institutes (SBIs)** are organized through the SBA on over 500 university and college campuses. At each SBI, on-site management counseling is provided by senior and graduate students at schools of business administration working with faculty advisors. In addition to counseling individual businesses, schools provide economic development assistance to communities. Students are guided by faculty advisors and SBA development staff and receive academic credit for their work.

◈ **Small Business Development Centers (SBDCs)** draw their resources from local, state, and federal government programs, the private sector, and university facilities. They provide managerial and technical help, research studies, and other types of specialized assistance. These centers are generally located or headquartered in academic institutions and provide individual counseling and practical training for small business owners. www.asbdc-us.org

◈ **Publications.** Business Development has over 100 business publications that are available for a nominal fee. They address the most important questions asked by prospective and existing business owners. A free copy of *Directory of Business Development Publications* can be obtained by contacting your local SBA office or by calling the Small Business Answer Desk at 800-827-5722.

Other Federal Resources

Many publications on business management and other related topics are available from the Government Printing Office (GPO). GPO bookstores are located in 24 major cities and are listed in the Yellow Pages under the "bookstore" heading. You can request a "Subject Bibliography" by writing to: Government Printing Office, Superintendent of Documents, Washington, DC 20402 or by phoning 202-783-3238. Information on government publications is also available at the Government Printing Office's site: www.gpo.gov/

Many federal agencies offer publications of interest to small businesses. There is a nominal fee for some, but most are free. Below is a partial list of government agencies that provide publications and other services targeted to small businesses. Information on publications can be obtained by phoning or writing the agency or by accessing their Web site.

U. S. Department of Agriculture
1400 Independence Avenue SW
Washington, DC 20250

Economic Research Service	202-694-5050
	www.econ.ag.gov/
National Agricultural Statistics Service	800-727-9540
	www.usda.gov/nass/

U. S. Department of Commerce
Washington, DC 20233

Bureau of the Census	301-457-4100
	www.census.gov/
Bureau of Economic Analysis	202-606-9900
	www.bea.doc.gov/
International Trade Administration	202-482-2185
	www.ita.doc.gov/tradestats/

U. S. Department of the Treasury
Internal Revenue Service   202-874-0410
Washington, DC 20013   www.irs.ustreas.gov/cover.html

U.S. Department of Labor
2 Massachusetts Avenue NE
Washington, DC 20212

Bureau of Labor Statistics	202-606-5886
	www.stats.bls.gov/
Employment and Training Administration	202-219-6871
	www.doleta.gov/

Environmental Protection Agency
Information Resource Center
401 M Street, SW   202-260-5922
Washington, DC 20460   www.epa.gov/

Copyright Office, LM 455
Library of Congress
Washington, DC 20559

202-707-3000 (Copyright Information Specialist)
202-707-9100 (Forms and circular requests)
www.lcweb.loc.gov/copyright/circs/

Patent and Trademark Office
Department of Commerce   703-557-4636
Washington, DC 20231   www.uspto.gov/

Associations and Agencies

Direct Marketing Association
11 West 42rd Street
New York, NY 10036   212-768-7277
                                          www.the-dma.org

Offers wide range of educational and information services to members
and the public.

National Association of Manufacturers
1331 Pennsylvania Avenue NW, Suite 1500 N
Washington, DC 20004   800-814-8468
                                                         www.nam.org

Membership-based association of manufacturing firms representing the interests of small manufacturers.

National Association of Women Business Owners (NAWBO)
1100 Wayne Avenue, Suite 830
Silver Springs, MD 20910   800-608-2595
                                                         www.nawbo.org

Membership-based organization offering workshops and seminars, providing information and referral services to members, and maintaining a database of women-owned businesses.

National Association for the Self-Employed
2121 Precinct Line Road
Dallas, TX 75261   800-232-6273
                                                         www.nase.org

Organization serving needs of small business owners. Helps owners obtain competitive employee benefits, offers discounts on items such as office equipment and telephone service, and provides a toll-free small business advice hotline.

National Federation of Independent Business
53 Century Boulevard, Suite 300
Nashville, TN 37214   800-634-2669
                                                         www.nfib.org

The country's largest small business association with more than 500,000 member business owners. In addition to representing small business interests to state and federal governments, it distributes educational information and publications, and holds conferences.

R.L. Polk
431 Howard Street
Detroit, MI 48231   800-635-5522
                                                         www.polk.com

Rents direct mail lists.

Books and Publications

Bade, Nicholas. *More Marketing without Money*. Willoughby, OH: Halle House Publishing, 1994.

Bangs, David, *The Market Planning Guide, 5th edition*. Chicago: Dearborn, 1998.

Bangs, David, and Linda Pinson. *The Real World Entrepreneur Field Guide*. Chicago: Dearborn, 1999.

Beckwith, Harry. *Selling the Invisible*. New York: Warner Books, Inc., 1997.

Blankenship, A.B., and George Breen. *State of the Art Marketing Research*. Chicago: NTC Business Books, 1998.

Clifford, Denis, and Ralph Warner. *The Partnership Book*. Berkeley, CA: Nolo Press, 1997.

Elias, Stephen. *A Dictionary of Patent, Copyright, and Trademark Terms*. Berkeley, CA: Nolo Press, 1991.

Fletcher, Tana. *Getting Publicity, 2nd edition*. Bellingham, WA: Self-Counsel Press, 1995.

Francese, Peter. *Marketing Know-How*. Ithaca NY: American Demographics Books, 1998.

Hall, Stephen. *From Kitchen to Market, 2nd edition*. Chicago: Dearborn, 1996.

Jones, Katina. *Businesses You Can Start Almanac*. Holbrook, MA: Adams Media Corp., 1996.

Levinson, Jay Conrad. *Guerrilla Marketing, 3rd edition*. Boston: Houghton-Mifflin, 1998.

Mosley, Thomas. *Marketing Your Invention, 2nd edition*. Chicago: Dearborn, 1997.

Pinson, Linda, and Jerry Jinnett. *Keeping the Books, 4th edition*. Chicago: Dearborn, 1998.

Pinson, Linda, and Jerry Jinnett. *Target Marketing, 3rd edition*. Chicago: Dearborn, 1996.

Pinson, Linda, and Jerry Jinnett. *Anatomy of a Business Plan, 4th edition*. Chicago: Dearborn, 1999.

Shenson, Howard, and Ted Nicholas. *The Complete Guide to Consulting Success, 3rd edition*. Chicago: Dearborn, 1997.

Steingold, Fred. *The Legal Guide for Starting and Running a Small Business*. Berkeley, CA: Nolo Press, 1998.

Library Resources

Bacon's Newspaper/Magazine Directory. Lists media as source of publicity information.

City and County Data Book. This book is updated every three years and contains statistical information on population, education, employment, income, housing, and retail sales.

Dun and Bradstreet Directories. Lists companies alphabetically, geographically, and by product classification.

Encyclopedia of Associations. Lists trade and professional associations throughout the United States. Many publish newsletters and provide marketing information. These associations can help business owners keep up with the latest industry developments.

Encyclopedia of Business Information Sources. Lists handbooks, periodicals, directories, trade associations, and more for over 1,200 specific industries and business subjects. Start here to search for information on your particular business.

Incubators for Small Business. Lists over 170 state government offices and incubators that offer financial and technical aid to new small businesses.

Lifestyle Market Analyst. Reference book published annually by R.L. Polk and Standard Rate and Data Service; contains demographic and psychographic stats for Metropolitan Statistical Areas in the entire United States.

National Trade and Professional Associations of the U.S. Trade and professional associations are indexed by association, geographic region, subject, and budget.

Reference Book for World Traders. This three-volume set lists banks, chambers of commerce, customs, marketing organizations, invoicing procedures, and more for 185 foreign markets. Sections on export planning, financing, shipping, laws, and tariffs are also included, with a directory of helpful government agencies.

Small Business Sourcebook. A good starting place for finding consultants, educational institutions, governmental agencies offering assistance, as well as specific information sources for over 140 types of businesses.

Sourcebook for Franchise Opportunities. Provides annual directory information for U.S. franchises, and data for investment requirements, royalty and advertising fees, services furnished by the franchiser, projected growth rates, and locations where franchises are licensed to operate.

U.S. Industrial Outlook. Provides an overview, forecasts, and short profiles for 200 American industries, including statistics on recent trends and a five-year outlook.

Worksheets

∙∙

Ready to Copy for Your Own Use

The blank forms and worksheets on the following pages have been provided for you to copy and use for your own business.

When you use the recordkeeping forms, you will notice that categories under fixed and variable expenses in the financial statements (profit & loss statement and cash flow statement) have been left blank. The categories are developed by using the categories from your revenue and expense journal. Those expenses that are frequent and/or sizable will have a heading of their own (i.e., advertising, rent, salaries, etc.). Those that are very small will be included under the heading "miscellaneous" in either the variable or fixed expense sections of each of your financial statements.

Personal Assessment Worksheet 1

Skills	Interests	Personal Qualities	Business Ideas

Personal Assessment Worksheet 2

Strengths	Weaknesses	Action Plan	Cost	Time

Buying a Business Worksheet

Name of business: _____

Type of business: _____

Address: _____

_____

Contact person: _____

Why is this business for sale? _____

What is the history of this business? _____

_____

Has this business been profitable? _____

_____

_____

_____

_____

What will I be buying? _____

   Accounts payable/liabilities: _____

   Accounts receivable: _____

   Business name: _____

_____

   Customer list: _____

   Fixed assets: _____

   Inventory: _____

   Lease: _____

   Personnel: _____

_____

   Proprietary rights (copyright, patent, trademark): _____

_____

   Unpaid taxes: _____

What is the selling price of this business? _____

How will I finance this purchase? _____

_____

Buying a Franchise Worksheet

Name of franchise: _____

Type of business: _____

_____

_____

Address: _____

Contact person: _____

What is the reputation of the franchisor? _____

_____

_____

Is the company involved in litigation? _____

_____

_____

What is the reputation of the individual business? _____

_____

_____

What training and start-up assistance is offered by the franchisor? _____

_____

_____

_____

What continuing assistance is offered by the franchisor? _____

_____

_____

_____

What is the management structure of the organization? _____

_____

_____

_____

Is the location and territory protected? _____

_____

_____

Buying a Franchise Worksheet, continued

What are the operating practices of the franchise? _____
_____
_____

What are the operating control policies? _____
_____
_____

What are the franchise costs? _____
_____
_____

Initial license fee: _____
_____
_____

Continuing royalty fees: _____
_____
_____

Other fees: _____
_____
_____

How will the sale be financed? _____
_____
_____

Do I have the right to sell the franchise? _____
_____
_____

What are the terms of renewal and termination? _____
_____
_____
_____
_____

Location Analysis Worksheet

1. Address: _____

2. Name, address, phone number of Realtor/contact person: _____
   _____

3. Square footage/cost: _____
   _____
   _____

4. History of location: _____
   _____
   _____

5. Location in relation to target market: _____
   _____
   _____

6. Traffic patterns for customers: _____
   _____
   _____

7. Traffic patterns for suppliers: _____
   _____
   _____

8. Availability of parking (include diagram): _____
   _____
   _____

9. Crime rate for the area: _____
   _____
   _____

10. Quality of public services (e.g., police, fire protection): _____
    _____
    _____

11. Notes from walking tour of the area: _____
    _____
    _____

Location Analysis Worksheet, continued

12. Neighboring shops and local business climate: _____

_____

_____

13. Zoning regulations: _____

_____

_____

14. Adequacy of utilities (get information from utility company representatives): _____

_____

_____

_____

15. Availability of raw materials/supplies: _____

_____

16. Availability of labor force: _____

_____

_____

17. Labor rate of pay for the area: _____

_____

_____

_____

18. Housing availability for employees: _____

_____

_____

_____

19. Tax rates (state, county, income, payroll, special assessments): _____

_____

_____

20. Evaluation of site in relation to competition: _____

_____

_____

_____

Choosing a Bank Worksheet

		Name of Potential Financial Institution		
		A.	B.	C.
1.	Have you already established a working relationship with: a. the management? b. the personnel?			
2.	What kind of business bank accounts are available?			
3.	Does this bank offer merchant credit card services?			
4.	Does the business participate in business loan programs?			
5.	Is the bank a federal depository bank?			
6.	Is the bank a stable financial institution?			
7.	How many branches does the bank have?			
8.	Is the location of the bank convenient for your business?			
9.	What are the bank's hours of operation? Are they open on Saturdays?			
10.	Will the bank place a holding period on your deposits?			
11.	What will it cost you to have a business checking account?			
12.	What other services does the bank have: a. electronic banking? b. safe deposit? c. notary public? d. electronic transfer? e. other?			
13.	What is your overall feeling about the bank?			

Insurance Update Form

Business Name: _____   **Updated as of** _____ ___, _____

	Company	Contact Person	Coverage	Cost Per Year
1.				$
2.				$
3.				$
4.				$
5.				$
6.				$
7.				$
1. TOTAL ANNUAL INSURANCE COST				$
2. AVERAGE MONTHLY INSURANCE COST				$

NOTES:

1.
2. .
3.

Revenue & Expense Journal

Month: _____ 20____, page ____

— Customize headings to match the business —

CHECK NO.	DATE	TRANSACTION	REVENUE	EXPENSE									MISC
		Balance forward---											
		TOTALS											

Petty Cash Record

PETTY CASH - 20___					Page ___
DATE	PAID TO WHOM	EXPENSE ACCOUNT DEBITED	DEPOSIT	AMOUNT OF EXPENSE	BALANCE
	BALANCE FORWARD				

Inventory Record
Non-Identifiable Stock

DEPARTMENT/CATEGORY:						

PRODUCTION OR PURCHASE DATE	INVENTORY PURCHASED OR MANUFACTURED		NUMBER OF UNITS	UNIT COST	VALUE ON DATE OF INVENTORY (Unit Cost X Units on Hand)	
	Stock #	Description			Value	Date

Inventory Record
Identifiable Stock

WHOLESALER:						Page____

PURCH DATE	INVENTORY PURCHASED		PURCH. PRICE	DATE SOLD	SALE PRICE	NAME OF BUYER (Optional)
	Stock #	Description				

Fixed Assets Log

COMPANY NAME: _____

ASSET PURCHASED	DATE PLACED IN SERVICE	COST OF ASSET	% USED FOR BUSINESS	RECOVERY PERIOD	METHOD OF DEPRECIATION	DEPRECIATION PREVIOUSLY ALLOWED	DATE SOLD	SALE PRICE

Accounts Payable
Account Record

CREDITOR: _____

ADDRESS: _____

_____

TEL. NO: _____   ACCOUNT NO._____

INVOICE DATE	INVOICE NO.	INVOICE AMOUNT		TERMS	DATE PAID	AMOUNT PAID		INVOICE BALANCE	

Accounts Receivable
Account Record

CUSTOMER:_____

ADDRESS: _____

_____

TEL. NO: _____   ACCOUNT NO._____

INVOICE DATE	INVOICE NO.	INVOICE AMOUNT	TERMS	DATE PAID	AMOUNT PAID	INVOICE BALANCE

Mileage Log

NAME: _____

DATED: From_____To_____

DATE	CITY OF DESTINATION	NAME OR OTHER DESIGNATION	BUSINESS PURPOSE	NO. OF MILES
			TOTAL MILES THIS SHEET	

Entertainment Expense Record

NAME: _____

DATED: From_____To_____

DATE	PLACE OF ENTERTAINMENT	BUSINESS PURPOSE	NAME OF PERSON ENTERTAINED	AMOUNT SPENT

Travel Record

Business Purpose: _____

No. Days Spent on Business _____

TRIP TO: _____

Dated From: _____ **To:** _____

| DATE | LOCATION | EXPENSE PAID TO | MEALS | | | HOTEL | TAXIS, ETC. | AUTOMOBILE | | | MISC EXP |
			Breakfast	Lunch	Dinner	Misc.			Gas	Parking	Tolls	
TOTALS →												

Balance Sheet

Business Name: _____   **Date:** _____ ___, _____

ASSETS

Current assets

Cash	$ _____
Petty cash	$ _____
Accounts receivable	$ _____
Inventory	$ _____
Short-term investments	$ _____
Prepaid expenses	$ _____

Long-term investments $ _____

Fixed assets

Land (valued at cost) $ _____

Buildings $ _____
  1. Cost   _____
  2. Less acc. depr.   _____

Improvements $ _____
  1. Cost   _____
  2. Less acc. depr.   _____

Equipment $ _____
  1. Cost   _____
  2. Less acc. depr.   _____

Furniture $ _____
  1. Cost   _____
  2. Less acc. depr.   _____

Autos/vehicles $ _____
  1. Cost   _____
  2. Less acc. depr.   _____

Other assets
  1. $ _____
  2. $ _____

TOTAL ASSETS $ _____

LIABILITIES

Current liabilities

Accounts payable	$ _____
Notes payable	$ _____
Interest payable	$ _____

Taxes payable
  Federal income tax $ _____
  Self-employment tax $ _____
  State income tax $ _____
  Sales tax accrual $ _____
  Property tax $ _____

Payroll accrual $ _____

Long-term liabilities
Notes payable $ _____

TOTAL LIABILITIES $ _____

NET WORTH (EQUITY)

Proprietorship $ _____
  or
Partnership
(name)_____, ___% equity $ _____
(name)_____, ___% equity $ _____
  or
Corporation
  Capital stock $ _____
  Surplus paid in $ _____
  Retained earnings $ _____

TOTAL NET WORTH $ _____

Assets – Liabilities = Net Worth
and
Liabilities + Equity = Total Assets

Profit & Loss (Income) Statement

Business Name: _____

Beginning: _____ ____, _____   **Ending:** _____ ____, _____

INCOME		
1. Sales revenues		$
2. Cost of goods sold (c – d)		
a. Beginning inventory (1/01)		
b. Purchases		
c. C.O.G. avail. sale (a + b)		
d. Less ending inventory (12/31)		
3. Gross profit on sales (1 – 2)		$
EXPENSES		
1. Variable (selling) (a thru h)		
a.		
b.		
c.		
d.		
e.		
f.		
g. Misc. variable (selling) expense		
h. Depreciation (prod/serv. assets)		
2. Fixed (administrative) (a thru h)		
a.		
b.		
c.		
d.		
e.		
f.		
g. Misc. fixed (administrative) expense		
h. Depreciation (office equipment)		
Total operating expenses (1 + 2)		
Net income from operations (GP – Exp)		$
Other income (interest income)		
Other expense (interest expense)		
Net profit (loss) before taxes		$
Taxes		
a. Federal		
b. State		
c. Local		
NET PROFIT (LOSS) AFTER TAXES		$

Cash to Be Paid Out Worksheet

Business Name: _____   **Time Period:** _____ **to** _____

1. START-UP COSTS   _____

    Business license

    Corporation filing   _____

    Legal fees   _____

    Other start-up costs: _____

       a.   _____

       b.   _____

       c.   _____

       d.   _____

2. INVENTORY PURCHASES

    Cash out for goods intended for resale   _____

3. VARIABLE EXPENSES (SELLING)

    a.   _____

    b.   _____

    c.   _____

    d.   _____

    e.   _____

    f.   _____

    g. Miscellaneous variable expense   _____

TOTAL SELLING EXPENSES   _____

4. FIXED EXPENSES (ADMINISTRATIVE)

    a.   _____

    b.   _____

    c.   _____

    d.   _____

    e.   _____

    f.   _____

    g. Miscellaneous fixed expense   _____

TOTAL ADMINISTRATIVE EXPENSE   _____

5. ASSETS (LONG-TERM PURCHASES)   _____

    Cash to be paid out in current period

6. LIABILITIES

    Cash outlay for retiring debts, loans

    and/or accounts payable   _____

7. OWNER EQUITY

    Cash to be withdrawn by owner   _____

TOTAL CASH TO BE PAID OUT $ _____

Sources of Cash Worksheet

Business Name: _____

Time Period Covered: _____ ___, _____ **to** _____ ___, _____

---

1. CASH ON HAND _____

2. SALES (REVENUES)

    Product sales income _____

    Services income _____

    Deposits on sales or services _____

    Collections on accounts receivable _____

3. MISCELLANEOUS INCOME

    Interest income

    Payments to be received on loans _____

4. SALE OF LONG-TERM ASSETS _____

5. LIABILITIES _____

    Loan funds (to be received during current period; from banks,
    through the SBA, or from other lending institutions)

6. EQUITY

    Owner investments (sole prop/partners) _____

    Contributed capital (corporation) _____

    Sale of stock (corporation) _____

    Venture capital _____

A. Without sales = $ _____

TOTAL CASH AVAILABLE

B. With sales = $ _____

Pro Forma Cash Flow Statement

Business Name: _____

Year: _____

	Jan	Feb	Mar	Apr	May	Jun	6-MONTH TOTALS	Jul	Aug	Sep	Oct	Nov	Dec	12-MONTH TOTALS
BEGINNING CASH BALANCE														
CASH RECEIPTS														
A. Sales/revenues														
B. Receivables														
C. Interest income														
D. Sale of long-term assets														
TOTAL CASH AVAILABLE														
CASH PAYMENTS														
A. Cost of goods to be sold														
1. Purchases														
2. Material														
3. Labor														
Total cost of goods														
B. Variable expenses														
1.														
2.														
3.														
4.														
5.														
6.														
7. Misc. variable expense														
Total variable expenses														
C. Fixed expenses														
1.														
2.														
3.														
4.														
5.														
6.														
7. Misc. fixed expense														
Total fixed expenses														
D. Interest expense														
E. Federal income tax														
F. Other uses														
G. Long-term asset payments														
H. Loan payments														
I. Owner draws														
TOTAL CASH PAID OUT														
CASH BALANCE/DEFFICIENCY														
LOANS TO BE RECEIVED														
EQUITY DEPOSITS														
ENDING CASH BALANCE														

Questionnaire Coding Log

Company: _____

Code	Date	Number Sent	Destination/ Recipient	Response Rate	Evaluation

Target Market Worksheet

1. Who are my customers?

   Profile: _____

   _____

   Economic level: _____

   _____

   Psychological make-up (lifestyle): _____

   _____

   Age range: _____

   Sex: _____

   Income level: _____

   _____

   Buying habits: _____

   _____

2. Where are my customers located?

   Where do they live: _____

   _____

   Where do they work: _____

   _____

   Where do they shop: _____

   _____

3. Projected size of the market:

   _____

   _____

   _____

   _____

   _____

   _____

Target Market Worksheet, continued

4. What are the customers needs?

_____

_____

_____

_____

_____

_____

_____

5. How can I meet those needs?

_____

_____

_____

_____

_____

_____

_____

6. What is unique about my business?

_____

_____

_____

_____

_____

_____

Market Research Worksheet

Questions	Information Source	Results	Effect on Plan

Competition Evaluation Form

1. Competitor: _____

2. Location: _____

   _____

3. Products or services offered: _____

4. Methods of distribution: _____

5. Image: _____

   Packaging: _____

   Promotional materials: _____

   Methods of advertising: _____

   Quality of product or service: _____

6. Pricing structure: _____

   _____

7. Business history and current performance: _____

   _____

8. Market share (number, types, and location of customers): _____

   _____

9. Strengths (the strengths of the competition become your strengths): _____

   _____

10. Weaknesses (looking at the weaknesses of the competition can help you find ways of being unique
    and of benefiting the customer): _____

    _____

    _____

    _____

    _____

    _____

Note: A Competition Evaluation Worksheet should be made for each competitor. Keep these records and update them. It pays to continue to rate your competition throughout the lifetime of your business.

Advertising Worksheet

Name of business: _____

1. What are the features and benefits of my product or service? _____
    _____
    _____
    _____

2. Who is my audience? _____
    _____
    _____
    _____

3. Who is my competition and how do they advertise? _____
    _____
    _____
    _____

4. What are the goals of my advertising campaign? _____
    _____
    _____
    _____

5. How much do I plan to invest for advertising? _____
    _____
    _____
    _____

6. What advertising methods will I use? _____
    __ Newspapers   __ Magazines   __ Yellow pages
    __ Radio   __ Television   __ Direct mail
    __ Telemarketing   __ Flyers   __ Brochures
    __ Coupons   __ Press release   __ Promo items
    __ Other _____

7. When will I use them and what will they cost? _____
    _____
    _____
    _____
    _____
    _____

8. How will I measure the effectiveness of the advertising plan? _____
    _____
    _____
    _____
    _____
    _____

Advertising Response Record

Company name: _____

Type of Ad	Date Run	Cost	Circulation	Number of Responses	Income Generated

Publicity Tracking Record

Company name: _____

Media Name	Contact Person	Address	Date	Material Sent	Follow-up	Response	Results	Notes

Glossary

· ·

account A record of a business transaction. A contract arrangement, written or unwritten, to purchase and take delivery with payment to be made later as arranged.

account balance The difference between the debit and the credit sides of an account.

accountant One who is skilled at keeping business records. Usually, a highly trained professional rather than one who keeps books. An accountant can set up the books needed for a business to operate and help the owner understand them.

accounting period A time interval at the end of which an analysis is made of the information contained in the bookkeeping records. Also the period of time covered by the profit and loss statement.

accounts payable Money you owe to an individual or business for goods or services that have been received but not yet paid for.

accounts receivable Money owed to your business for goods or services that have been delivered but not yet paid for.

accrual basis A method of keeping accounts that shows expenses incurred and income earned for a given fiscal period, even though such expenses and income have not been actually paid or received in cash.

actuary A professional expert in pension and life insurance matters, particularly trained in mathematical, statistical, and accounting methods and procedures, and in insurance probabilities.

administrative expense Expenses chargeable to the managerial, general administrative, and policy phases of a business in contrast to sales, manufacturing, or cost of goods expense.

advertising The practice of bringing to the public's notice the good qualities of something in order to induce the public to buy or invest in it.

agent A person who is authorized to act for or represent another person in dealing with a third party.

· · · · · ·

amortization To liquidate on an installment basis; the process of gradually paying off a liability over a period of time.

analysis Breaking an idea or problem down into its parts; a thorough examination of the parts of anything.

annual report The yearly report made by a company at the close of the fiscal year, stating the company's receipts and disbursements, assets, and liabilities.

appraisal Evaluation of a specific piece of personal or real property. The value placed on the property evaluated.

appreciation The increase in the value of an asset in excess of its depreciable cost due to economic and other conditions, as distinguished from increases in value due to improvements or additions made to it.

arrears Amounts past due and unpaid.

Articles of Incorporation A legal document filed with the state that sets forth the purposes and regulations for a corporation. Each state has different regulations.

assets Anything of worth that is owned. Accounts receivable are an asset.

audiotaping The act of recording onto an audio tape.

audit An examination of accounting documents and of supporting evidence for the purpose of reaching an informed opinion concerning their propriety.

bad debts Money owed to you that you cannot collect.

balance The amount of money remaining in an account.

balance sheet An itemized statement that lists the total assets and total liabilities of a given business to portray its net worth at a given moment in time.

bank statement A monthly statement of account which a bank renders to each of its depositors.

benchmarking Rating your company's products, services, and practices against those of the front-runners in the industry.

bill of lading A document issued by a railroad or other carrier. It acknowledges the receipt of specified goods for transportation to a certain place, it sets forth the contract between the shipper and the carrier, and it provides for proper delivery of the goods.

bill of sale Formal legal document that conveys title to or interest in specific property from the seller to the buyer.

board of directors Those individuals elected by the stockholders of a corporation to manage the business.

bookkeeping The process of recording business transactions into the accounting records. The "books" are the documents where the records of transactions are kept.

bottom line The figure that reflects company profitability on the income statement. The bottom line is the profit after all expenses and taxes have been paid.

brand A design, mark, symbol, or other device that distinguishes one line or type of goods from those of a competitor.

brand name A term, symbol, design, or combination thereof that identifies and differentiates a seller's products or service.

breakeven The point of business activity when total revenue equals total expenses. Above the breakeven point, the business is making a profit. Below the breakeven point, the business is incurring a loss.

budget An estimate of the income and expenditures for a future period of time, usually one year.

business venture Taking financial risks in a commercial enterprise.

capital Money available to invest or the total of accumulated assets available for production.

capital equipment Equipment you use to manufacture a product, provide a service or use to sell, store, and deliver merchandise. Such equipment will not be sold in the normal course of business, but will be used and worn out or consumed in the course of business.

capital gains (and losses) The difference between purchase price and selling price in the sale of assets.

cash Money in hand or readily available.

cash discount A deduction that is given for prompt payment of a bill.

cash flow The actual movement of cash within a business; the analysis of how much cash is needed and when that money is required by a business within a period of time.

cash receipts The money received by a business from customers.

Certified Public Accountant (CPA) An accountant who has met prescribed requirements designed to ensure competence on the part of the public practitioner in accounting as directed by the state. The designation is that of a Certified Public Accountant, commonly abbreviated as CPA.

chamber of commerce An organization of business people designed to advance the interests of its members. There are three levels: national, state, and local.

choice A decision to purchase that is based on an evaluation of alternatives.

co-signers Joint signers of a loan agreement who pledge to meet the obligations of a business in case of default.

collateral Something of value given or held as a pledge that a debt or obligation will be fulfilled.

commission A percentage of the principal or of the income that an agent receives as compensation for services.

contract An agreement regarding mutual responsibilities between two or more parties.

controllable expenses Those expenses that can be controlled or restrained by the business person.

corporation A voluntary organization of persons, either actual individuals or legal entities, legally bound together to form a business enterprise; an artificial legal entity created by government grant and treated by law as an individual entity.

cost of goods sold The direct cost to the business owner of those items which will be sold to customers.

credit Another word for debt. Credit is given to customers when they are allowed to make a purchase with the promise to pay later. A bank gives credit when it lends money.

credit line The maximum amount of credit or money a financial institution or trade firm will extend to a customer.

current assets Valuable resources or property owned by a company that will be turned into cash within one year or used up in the operations of the company within one year. Generally includes cash, accounts receivable, inventory, and prepaid expenses.

current liabilities Amounts owed that will ordinarily be paid by a company within one year. Generally includes accounts payable, current portion of long-term debt, interest, and dividends payable.

debt That which is owed. Debt refers to borrowed funds and is generally secured by collateral or a co-signer.

debt capital The part of the investment capital that must be borrowed.

default The failure to pay a debt or meet an obligation.

deficit The excess of liabilities over assets; a negative net worth.

depreciation A decrease in value through age, wear, or deterioration. Depreciation is a normal expense of doing business that must be taken into account. There are laws and regulations governing the manner and time periods that may be used for depreciation.

desktop publishing Commonly used term for computer-generated printed materials such as newsletters and brochures.

differentiated marketing Selecting and developing a number of offerings to meet the needs of a number of specific market segments.

direct mail Marketing goods or services directly to the consumer through the mail.

direct selling The process whereby the producer sells to the user, ultimate consumer, or retailer without intervening middlemen.

discount A deduction from the stated or list price of a product or service.

distribution channel All of the individuals and organizations involved in the process of moving products from producer to consumer. The route a product follows as it moves from the original grower, producer, or importer to the ultimate consumer.

distributor Middleman, wholesaler, agent, or company distributing goods to dealers or companies.

downsize Term currently used to indicate employee reassignment, layoffs and restructuring in order to make a business more competitive, efficient, and/or cost-effective.

entrepreneur An innovator of business enterprise who recognizes opportunities to introduce a new product, a new process, or an improved organization, and who raises the necessary money, assembles the factors for production, and organizes an operation to exploit the opportunity.

equipment Physical property of a more or less permanent nature ordinarily useful in carrying on operations, other than land, buildings, or improvements to either of them. Examples are machinery, tools, trucks, cars, ships, furniture, and furnishings.

equity A financial investment in a business. An equity investment carries with it a share of ownership of the business, a stake in the profits, and a say in how it is managed. Equity is calculated by subtracting the liabilities of the business from the assets of the business.

equity capital Money furnished by owners of the business.

exchange The process where two or more parties give something of value to one another to satisfy needs and wants.

facsimile machine (fax) Machine capable of transmitting written input via telephone lines.

financial statements Documents that show your financial situation.

fixed expenses Those costs that don't vary from one period to the next. Generally, these expenses are not affected by the volume of business. Fixed expenses are the basic costs that every business will have each month.

franchise Business that requires three elements: franchise fee, common trade name, and continuous relationship with the parent company.

fundraising Events staged to raise revenue.

gross profit The difference between the selling price and the cost of an item. Gross profit is calculated by subtracting cost of goods sold from net sales.

guarantee A pledge by a third party to repay a loan in the event that the borrower cannot.

home page The "table of contents" to a Web site, detailing what pages are on a particular site. The first page one sees when accessing a Web site.

income statement A financial document that shows how much money (revenue) came in and how much money (expense) was paid out.

interest The cost of borrowing money.

Internet The vast collection in inter-connected networks that provide electronic mail and access to the World Wide Web.

inventory A list of assets being held for sale.

invest To lay out money for any purpose where a profit is expected.

keystone Setting a retail price at twice the wholesale price.

lead The name and address of a possible customer.

lease A long-term rental agreement.

liability insurance Risk protection for actions where a business is liable.

license Formal permission to conduct business.

lifestyle A pattern of living that comprises an individual's activities, interests, and opinions.

limited partnership A legal partnership where some owners are allowed to assume responsibility only up to the amount invested.

liquidity The ability of a business to meet its financial responsibilities. The degree of readiness where assets can be converted into cash without loss.

loan agreement A document that states what a business can and cannot do as long as it owes money to the lender.

loan Money lent with interest.

long-term liabilities The liabilities (expenses) that will not mature within the next year.

management The art of conducting and supervising a business.

market A set of potential or real buyers or a place where there is a demand for products or services. Actual or potential buyers of a product or service.

market demand Total volume purchased in a specific geographic area by a specific customer group in a specified time period under a specified marketing program.

market forecast An anticipated demand that results from a planned marketing expenditure.

market niche A well-defined group of customers that are interested in what you have to offer.

market positioning Finding a market niche that emphasizes the strengths of a product or service in relation to the weaknesses of the competition.

market share A company's percentage share of total sales within a given market.

market targeting Choosing a marketing strategy in terms of competitive strengths and marketplace realities.

marketing mix The set of product, place, promotion, price, and packaging variables, which a marketing manager controls and orchestrates to bring a product or service into the marketplace.

marketing research The systematic design, collection, analysis, and reporting of data regarding a specific marketing situation.

mass marketing Selecting and developing a single offering for an entire market.

merchandise Goods bought and sold in a business. "Merchandise" or stock is a part of inventory.

microbusiness An owner-operated business with few employees and less than $250,000 in annual sales.

middleman A person or company that performs functions or renders services involved in the purchase and/or sale of goods in their flow from producer to consumer.

multi-level sales Also known as network marketing. Rather than hiring sales staff, multilevel sales companies sell their products through thousands of independent distributors. Multi-level sales companies offer distributors commissions on both retail sales and the sales of their "downline" (the network of other distributors they sponsor).

need A state of perceived deprivation.

net What is left after deducting all expenses from the gross.

net worth The total value of a business in financial terms. Net worth is calculated by subtracting total liabilities from total assets.

niche A well-defined group of customers for which what you have to offer is particularly suitable.

nonrecurring One time; not repeating. Nonrecurring expenses are those involved in starting a business, and which only have to be paid once and will not occur again.

note A document that is recognized as legal evidence of a debt.

operating costs Expenditures arising out of current business activities. The costs incurred to do business such as salaries, electricity, and rental. Also may be called "overhead."

organizational market A marketplace made up of producers, trade industries, governments, and institutions.

outsourcing Term used in business to identify the process of sub-contracting work to outside vendors.

overhead A general term for costs of materials and services not directly adding to or readily identifiable with the product or service being sold.

partnership A legal business relationship of two or more people who share responsibilities, resources, profits, and liabilities.

payable Ready to be paid. One of the standard accounts kept by a bookkeeper is "accounts payable." This is a list of those bills that are current and due to be paid.

perception The process of selecting, organizing, and interpreting information received through the senses.

prepaid expenses Expenditures that are paid in advance for items not yet received.

price The exchange value of a product or service from the perspective of both the buyer and the seller.

price ceiling The highest amount a customer will pay for a product or a service based on perceived value.

price floor The lowest amount a business owner can charge for a product or service and still meet all expenses.

price planning The systematic process for establishing pricing objectives and policies.

principal The amount of money borrowed in a debt agreement and the amount interest is calculated on.

pro forma A projection or estimate of what may result in the future from actions in the present. A pro forma financial statement is one that shows how the actual operations of the business will turn out if certain assumptions are achieved.

producers The components of the organizational market that acquire products, services that enter into the production of products, and services that are sold or supplied to others.

product Anything capable of satisfying needs, including tangible items, services, and ideas.

product life cycle (PLC) The stages of development and decline through which a successful product typically moves.

product line A group of products related to each other by marketing, technical, or end-use considerations.

product mix All of the products in a seller's total product line.

profit and loss statement A list of the total amount of sales (revenues) and total costs (expenses). The difference between revenues and expenses is your profit or loss.

profit Financial gain, returns over expenditures.

profit margin The difference between your selling price and all of your costs.

promotion The communication of information by a seller to influence the attitudes and behavior of potential buyers.

promotional pricing Temporarily pricing a product or service below list price or below cost in order to attract customers.

psychographics The system of explaining market behavior in terms of attitudes and life styles.

publicity Any non-paid, news-oriented presentation of a product, service, or business entity in a mass media format.

quantitative forecasts Forecasts that are based on measurements of numerical quantities.

questionnaire A data-gathering form used to collect information by a personal interview, with a telephone survey, or through the mail.

ratio The relationship of one thing to another. A ratio is a short-cut way of comparing things, which can be expressed as numbers or degrees.

receivable Ready for payment. When you sell on credit, you keep an accounts receivable ledger as a record of what is owed to you and who owes it. In accounting, a receivable is an asset.

retail Selling directly to the consumer.

retailing Businesses and individuals engaged in the activity of selling products to final consumers.

revenue Total sales during a stated period.

sales potential A company's expected share of a market as marketing expenditures increase in relation to the competition.

sales promotion Marketing activities that stimulate consumer purchasing in the short term.

sales representative An independent salesperson who directs efforts to selling your products or service to others but is not an employee of your company. Sales reps often represent more than one product line from more than one company and usually work on commission.

sample A limited portion of the whole of a group.

security Collateral that is promised to a lender as protection in case the borrower defaults on a loan.

service business A retail business that deals in activities for the benefit of others.

share One of the equal parts that the ownership of a corporation is divided into. A share represents part ownership in a corporation.

short-term notes Loans that come due in one year or less.

sole proprietorship Business legal structure where one individual owns the business.

stock An ownership share in a corporation; another name for a share. Another definition would be accumulated merchandise.

suppliers Individuals or businesses that provide resources needed by a company in order to produce goods and services.

survey A research method in which people are asked questions.

takeover The acquisition of one company by another.

target market The specific individuals, distinguished by socio-economic, demographic, and interest characteristics, who are the most likely potential customers for the goods and services of a business.

target marketing Selecting and developing a number of offerings to meet the needs of a number of specific market segments.

telemarketing Marketing goods or services directly to the consumer via the telephone.

terms of sale The conditions concerning payment for a purchase.

trade credit Permission to buy from suppliers on open account.

undifferentiated marketing Selecting and developing one offering for an entire market.

venture capital Money invested in enterprises that do not have access to traditional sources of capital.

volume An amount or quantity of business; the volume of a business is the total it sells over a period of time.

wholesaling Businesses and individuals engaged in the activity of selling products to retailers, organizational users, or other wholesalers. Selling for resale.

working capital The excess of current assets over current liabilities. The cash needed to keep the business running from day to day.

Index

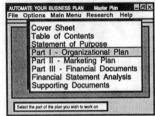
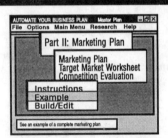
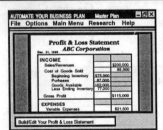